A Windy Hill Almanac

~MIKE LUNSFORD~

To Dudley,

A good man & better friend...

Thanks...

- 2014 -

Shade Tree Press

8945 South Coxville Rd.

Rosedale, Indiana 47874

www.mikelunsford.com

Printed in the United States of America

The author and publisher gratefully acknowledges the *Terre Haute Tribune-Star* in which the contents of this book appeared in column form.

Library of Congress Control Number: 2013902247

Front cover art, "Hillside of Whitetop and Daises," by Carl Graf, courtesy of Steve Aker and Vicki Timm. Inside cover art, courtesy of Page Fetter. Author's photo by Joan Lunsford.

Lunsford, Michael J. (Mike), 1956-
A Windy Hill Almanac/Mike Lunsford
ISBN 978-0-615-76553-2 (pbk.)

To all those who teach children, and to those who appreciate how hard it can be...

-Prologue-
-A Windy Hill in December-

It is a windy day in December as I write this; it is, in fact, just one day after Christmas, a half-dozen or so since the world was to end, according to the Mayans, but, we are still here. The snow has been blowing horizontally for hours now, since before the sun and I got out of bed to drink coffee and work a crossword puzzle together, me inside at the kitchen table, he outside trying his best to warm an icy day. The weatherman says we are to have a blizzard today, but I have seen little more than a regular, everyday snow storm, which I enjoy since the Welshman in me favors the occasional gray and white day.

The wind is almost always blowing across my place here in the Indiana countryside, so often, in fact, that I decided a long while ago to give this book its title in honor of it. Nearly a year ago, I wrote a story about our wind, and I included in the piece a favorite passage by Ernie Pyle about the winds of the Midwest. He said they blew in a "symphony of sadness," which they do, it seems to me, in the Hoosier fall when I hear the breeze rattling through the corn stalks of a dry and lifeless field. That sort of wind sounds pretty lonely as I hear it slipping through the leaves of our shingle oaks. All of our trees, except those, drop their leaves at once, and I rake them up before the fall is over. The wind reminds me, I guess, that not everything is so obedient to my want of convenience.

Our wind has multiple personalities. I am, at nearly the same time, afraid of it, yet I long for it too. Just last summer, as we endured a drought of historic proportions, we wanted the wind to blow, to ruffle our curtains and cool us off for a day or two, and to bring us a shower and the smell of leaves and grass. Instead, we got a daily sirocco, the super-heated whirlwinds of a blast furnace. Not until late fall did we get what we really wanted, and those glorious fresh winds, which rode the rails here all the way from Canada, have been replaced too soon by a "Siberian express."

Our wind is often welcome in the heat of the summer. Our house is situated in such a way that in the doldrums of August, we can always catch a breeze from beneath our big maples to the west. If we want to turn off the air conditioning and open our windows, the wind will most often blow right through the house and out into our back yard. On most days, I can be at work up the valley road from our place and not feel much of a wind there, but get me to the top of our ridge, and I can hear it and feel it, and take comfort in it as it moves through a chime or rattles the grit in the gutters. We've also learned to fear it as it throws itself at us from the fields that roll away from us just a few feet west of the road on which we live. In the winter it is switchblade sharp, so brutal that it piles the snow up against our doors as if moved by a bulldozer.

Obviously, this book isn't actually an almanac at all. It has no weather forecasts, no information about the tides, no planting advice. It's simply organized into four chapters named for the seasons, the stories in each about life in some way or another on this windy knob of a hill that sits in the southern end of a rolling central Indiana county. The word "almanac" (an archaic usage is spelled "almanack") has disputed origins. Ultimately, it may be Greek, and it may have meant "calendar." That suits my book's title just fine, but there's a better reason I went with the name I have. One synonym for almanac is "reminiscence," and in that activity I am often involved.

Not too long ago, I wrote a story about handwriting, and the importance of putting things down on paper, and how it helps in the development of our brains. I had my handwriting analyzed—with some trepidation—and one thing I was told intrigued me. According to the expert, my scribbling suggests that I look to the past for "reflection and guidance." That analysis is quite true, and the stories in this book will bear witness to it.

Ironically, I am writing this, the first pages of the book, last. All of the heavy lifting was done as I researched and wrote the stories in it as newspaper columns, week after week after week over the past few years. Oh, I've gone back through and hacked a little deadwood out where it was needed, and all kinds of formatting and editing were required to get this book—my fourth—together for you, but it wasn't written from scratch in one spate of inspiration. I think I'm going to have to retire from my regular job to ever get that kind of writing done.

As is usual, I have people to thank before I move on, and it is a familiar cast of characters if you have read my previous books. All of the stories here were once published in the "Terre Haute Tribune-Star," and so, my thanks go to the good folks there who helped my words first find their way into print. Specifically, publisher B.J. Riley, editors Max Jones and Susan Duncan, and feature writer Mark Bennett, get my usual nods of appreciation.

I want to also thank Stephen Mace Aker and his wife, Vicki Timm. They graciously supplied the beautiful art that graces the front of this book, Carl Graf's "Hillside of Whitetop and Daisies," a painting Steve's parents, Mace and Betty, bought many years ago in the hills of Brown County. My book is better for that picture, as it is for the art that appears on the inside cover page and book's spine. A talented student of mine, Page Fetter, drew it for me, and for her eye on the world I am most grateful.

And, finally, I once again need to thank my wife, Joanie. I have depended on her for help in just about everything good I have ever done in this life, and this book, I hope, is no exception.   ML

-Table of Contents-

Chapter 1: Winter

Chapter 2: Spring

Chapter 3: Summer

Chapter 4: Fall

"Everything changes, and nothing remains still... and you cannot step twice into the same stream."

Heraculitus

"Life's a voyage that's homeward bound."

Herman Melville

"Love what you do, and do what you love."

Ray Bradbury

~Winter~

"What good is the warmth of summer, without the cold of winter to give it sweetness." John Steinbeck

A house with a hearth becomes a home
December 12, 2011

My son came home with a load of wood one day last week. Our little two-wheeled mowing trailer was groaning under the oppressive weight it held, its tires as pudgy as a glutton's belly and its tongue nearly lapping the ground. He had to cut a few trees near our churchyard, hoping to prevent cleaning up an even bigger mess later on, and rather than just rolling the wood over the hill or letting it rot where it fell, he thought we could use it ourselves. His soon-to-be father-in-law, appropriately nicknamed "Moose," helped him cut and load the great chunks for hauling. I think the pair just wanted to do their weightlifting that day someplace other than in a sweaty gym.

Evan has been in the mood for hard work lately, and not the kind he finds behind a desk or the wheel of a car. At 24 he seeks out physical challenges like I used to, and, as of late, he's been splitting wood as if he had beaver blood running in his veins. With a maul and a wedge, an axe and an attitude, he tackled the load that same afternoon, swinging his tools of destruction as if his life depended on it. In less than two hours I had a cord of perfectly split white oak sitting under the protection of a massive pine along our driveway; it will last us a long time, particularly since I have another stack—this one larger—residing under the eaves of my old barn. I split most of that load — sycamore and maple and walnut, mostly—although Evan decided just a few weeks ago to knock the rust off my old tools and whack a little elm and add a row or two to it.

We don't have a wood burning stove at our place, although I've considered one for back-up when the power goes down.

We have a fireplace, which has come in handy many times when the juice no longer runs through our wires, but for the most part, we pick our spots through the winter to build a fire and play board games and watch movies and eat popcorn. It is a pleasant arrangement.

I grew tired of heating with wood from my days at home. My dad put a woodstove in when I was in my teens, and it seemed like all I did in those days was haul ashes out or bring new supply wood into an always-empty box. On some days our living room was as hot as a blast furnace, and I recall that on occasion my mom would have a window open just to bleed off some of the excess heat. But I will say that on a cold, cold day, standing next to that stove was a most pleasing thing. We all felt like old cats, curled up around the stove as it cracked and steamed.

Before that, our fireplace, built with the house over 60 years ago now, was an open affair, lined outside with rough red bricks and topped with a mantel of pine. In those days we had a gas "log" that we lit with a match. The burner had no faux logs around it, and it didn't crackle like many do now. It really just hissed at us as we huddled around its relatively low blue-yellow flames, most often in flannel and cotton, freshly clean from our baths and ready for bed.

My wife grew up with a fireplace too. Like my childhood hearth, it wasn't really built for show. Decades older than the one I grew up with, it was constructed around 1870 in the Italiante style farmhouse six miles up the road from my home. Sometime in the early '60s, her dad had a stone mason from Clinton come to the house and build a right proper hearth of pink and tan sandstone. Its firebox still holds the same ancient bricks it did when Ulysses Grant was president, and I remember that her dad, Gib, held court in front of that old fireplace at a lifetime of Thanksgivings and Christmases as his sons-in-law and grandkids watched the coal he fed into it glow. Those were good times too.

The fireplace in my living room is much older than our house. The hearth is made of wonderfully grained oak, and a mirror above the ancient mantel is surrounded by a pair of posts and intricate scrolled carving. I am told that the mantel came from a much older farmhouse up the road to the north of us; that homestead blew apart in a storm years and years ago, and when my house was built in the late 1950s, the mantel, probably minus the ceramic tile that was popular in such pieces in the first few decades of the last century, came to live in our house. We're glad it did.

Over the years, that hearth has been the fulcrum of our home. We have stood alongside one another in front of it for photos, stretched out before it to read our favorite books, slept beside it with a cold winter wind howling against a powerless house. My absolute favorite photo of my daughter is of her standing in front of that hearth, in pink and pigeon-toed and in an Easter bonnet. It has always been a tradition to hang our Christmas stockings from it, and who knows, in a few years, perhaps we'll be hanging a few more for grandchildren.

In just days, my son will be a married man. He will move away from our house to a place of his own. He has told me that in the future, he wants a fireplace and that the new maul and axe he owns will come in handy as he feeds it the wood it craves.

That is a good thing. I think a family needs a center, a hearth and its warmth, to turn to when the world outside is cold.

The more things change, the more they keep changing
December 26, 2011

I must have had at least a dozen people ask at my son's wedding a few weeks ago whether I cried, or "how I was handling losing him." I think they all knew just how tight I am with my two kids, and thought I must have come completely unglued when it finally hit me that he was on his own for good, that the rules had changed nearly a much in my life when he said, "I do," as they did for him.

"It's not like he's moving very far," I told more than one concerned friend. "I imagine he'll be at our kitchen table for a meal or two before long," I said. Above all, I didn't want to seem to be a panicked "empty nester," someone who is so wrapped up in his kids that he can't go on and live his own life, and I'm reasonably certain that the last thing my son wants his mom and me to do is sit in our house in nervous anticipation of a phone call or pop-in from the newlyweds.

I remained reasonably stoic that Saturday. "I don't cry at weddings," I bragged, and I joked that for the first time in my life I was going to be guaranteed a bathroom all to myself, that I wouldn't be lugging his enormous shoes out of my way anymore, that I wouldn't have to deal with a mangled toothpaste tube every morning. Why, my grocery bill will no longer require a search for loose change under the sofa cushions, and he won't be borrowing my dress socks anymore. He sometimes had no idea what he had done with the tools he'd borrowed, and my house is going to be quieter, I've thought. After all, Evan is a notorious door-slammer, hard walker, and table drummer.

I have to admit that I did get a little teary-eyed when I saw my son turn to see his bride coming down the aisle. I thought at the time that he had the same dumbfounded expression on his face that I had on mine over 30 years ago on my wedding day. Until that moment for each of us, I don't think we had truly realized how lucky we really were. And, when I saw a series of old snapshots of Evan with the three grandparents he's lost as they were flashed on a big church video screen, I did cry a bit, all in wishing that my folks and my wife's dad had lived long enough to see the day. I saw my son in football uniforms and with his 4-H rabbits and standing with my buddy, Joe, after a day of fishing, and it just hit me that each of those days was gone, not just for him, but for me too.

I also think I knew then that when it comes to the moment his sister marries, I won't stand a chance; like a lot of other dads, I'll just be a little puddle of water on the floor.

More than anything, I realized that the old adage that says that the "more things change, the more they stay the same," is mostly wrong. Life is change, and there's nothing we can do about it but ride its wave.

I don't want to make this too maudlin; I'm happy for my boy. He has a great girl, and he has a job, and he can take care of himself if he has to. He married into a good family and will have a tight roof over his head. Other than worrying about things that dads always worry about until the day they die, like whether he's saving instead of spending and if he's cleaning his water heater with regularity and checking his furnace filters, I'm pretty confident that we've raised a kid who will do the job of living a good life, so my tears were temporary.

I have already noticed in these past few days that

when I want to use the bathroom, Evan's not showering, that my toothpaste tube remains pristine, that there's room for my shoes by the backdoor, and that when Joanie came home from the grocery store yesterday the only reason we had a pretty hefty receipt is that she had bought a few extra bags worth of food to stick in the kids' refrigerator until they get their supply built up.

The house sure seems quiet though...

Windy companion gives writer the cold shoulder

January 9, 2012

The wind came to visit us this week. We live on the knob of a hill that overlooks a Raccoon Creek valley, and it is a breezy spot year-round, but this wind was the kind that ushers in a full-blown front from Canada, perhaps just to remind us that cold weather is going to be the boss around here for a while. No matter how surprising our mild winter has been so far, this kind of wind tells us not to expect many more warm days over the next few months.

Joanie and I noticed the wind at our place on the first day we came to live here. It was a breezy August afternoon, and since we had no air conditioning then, we had all of our windows open to catch the crosswinds that blew in under our maples, through the living room, and on out across the back hill to the woods below. We have, for most part, been friends ever since, particularly on those days when our wind chimes sing to us in the afternoons and early evenings and the winds are lazy and slow.

But last Sunday morning, after a surprisingly calm New Year's Eve that saw us warming our house with only a wood box of sassafras and oak and a fireplace, we heard the wind come in like a freight train, and the tune our front porch chimes played that night was as harsh as any dissonant symphony ever recorded. That wind was a mean left hook out of the north, and it left us a bit disappointed. I had to take the chimes down, and found pieces of two lying in a flower bed where the wind had dropped them.

Today, as I write this, I can see the wind, not just hear it. It is moving fat flakes of snow, a bit of which I noticed already accumulating near my cabin door when I came outside. My heater hasn't shut itself off for even a minute as the three big sycamore trees I watch through my window sway and rock from side to side.

The gray squirrel, who has built a rather impressive condo atop one of them, has to either be rocking in his sleep or a bit nauseous by now.

I think I brought a bit of this on myself. Just a few days ago, after a morning in town, my wife and I came home in the early afternoon to take down our outdoor Christmas decorations. I worked in shirt sleeves that day as we packed away lights and artificial trees and wreaths. More than once, I commented on how nice my yard looked, that there wasn't a single twig or limb down, that the grass was still fairly green, and that the decorations we always leave up well past Christmas — mostly red bows and green garlands — were still in place.

This morning, as I hunkered down in a heavy jacket and ball cap and gloves, I wandered the yard, stomping on bits of ribbon and silk poinsettias and a wreath or two before they blew over the hill. My nose ran and my cheeks grew red, as if I'd been slapped, as I also picked up a brass-colored sun that usually hangs as an optimistic symbol on the west side of the house above the porch; I'll return it to its proper place when it feels safe to climb a ladder again. Rounding the corner of my house, I noticed that the wind had knocked a birdhouse we keep for decoration off the back deck, too, and that the plastic I had used to cover a Mexican terracotta oven we keep near our door had been displaced, as if the wind had blown up a modest lady's skirt.

I found a roofing shingle in the yard. It didn't surprise me; we are planning to re-roof our house next spring, deciding to patch the worst spots and wait for safer, drier weather. I knew exactly where the shingle came from; I have tarred and glued and nailed in that place, a little promontory on our porch that bears the brunt of the northwest winds stoically, many times. But it often needs my help now, so I went to the barn to retrieve my roofing cement, a black goop that sets up like concrete in cold weather. I set the can near a register in the house to warm it, and plan to be on the roof later in the week.

The stiff breezes had knocked our trellis over too. Weighted down by two big chucks of sandstone and a bit of wire, it shivered so hard in the wind that it pulled itself apart at its base and flopped over into a dormant flower bed. I'll have to screw it back together when the wind stops. While I'm at it, I'll pick up a wheelbarrow or two of sticks and twigs too. Our maples seem to save them up for such a wind, then drop them all when I've gotten cocky and satisfied that my yard is clean.

Sitting here in the warmth, amidst the smell of books and coffee, I observed one of our barn cats as it hunkered down on the corner of our deck, its back to the wind. She had her eye on one of our birdfeeders and a fat cardinal that sat next to an ear of corn, hanging onto the wood with a death grip lest it blow away in a chaos of red feathers. Just a few days ago, he and his bird buddies sat in casual groups, enjoying the warmth of southern breezes and eating at leisure. Today, he was making a mad dash for a kernel or two before heading to the shelter of a brush pile behind my barn.

I also watched a pair of deer wander below me in the woods. Both were picking at the remains of a few Halloween pumpkins we tossed over the hill a while back. They didn't seem to be in a hurry to come up to the top of the ridge where they would have to face the harsh wind. How they make it through the winter nights like the one we are going to have tonight, I don't know. For their sake, and mine, I hope the weatherman is right when he says that warmer air is on its way, probably riding in on winds from the south.

One of my favorite passages in all of literature comes from Ernie Pyle. I have used it in this space before. In an essay about Indiana, Pyle spoke of the Midwestern winds, how they rustled "the leaves and the branches of the maple trees in a sort of symphony of sadness."

He was speaking of summer winds, not the same kind we're facing today. Sad as they may be, I'd take those winds — and open windows and singing wind chimes — over those of this January deep freeze. The cardinals would probably agree.

Hoping to master the art of taking a nap
January 23, 2012

I got away from work as early as I could one day last week. It was a cloudy day, filled with grayness and rain, and my head felt as if I had inhaled my pillow the night before. My throat suggested I'd swallowed a wood rasp, and my eyes felt as though I was looking through someone else's glasses. Yet, I had work do, this column being on the list of chores.

I made it home and through the front door, crawled out of my teacher duds and into a pair of jeans, plowed through our kitchen's medicine shelf to see if I could find a miracle drug that would make me feel better, and headed out to my cabin desk and chair, which on that day was about as inviting as a bed of nails.

Plodding along my keyboard at a sloth's pace, I considered taking a nap and leaving the writing to another time, perhaps another day altogether. I simply wanted to drop what I was doing, head to the house, furl myself into a corner of our family room, and drift off. I thought it would do me a great deal of good to have shut my eyes for a while. I think it would help all of us to do the same every now and again. Eventually, I let my story, the teetering stack of ungraded papers, and a few other odd jobs go undone. I moped to the house and grabbed a half-hour of sleep, knowing that the way I felt, the down time wouldn't disturb my night's rest at all.

I hope to someday master the art of napping, and I have good reasons. For instance, I recently read a piece in "Newsweek" titled "31 Ways to Get Smarter-Faster," and coming in at No. 6 was "Sleep, A Lot." Who am I to argue with science? Who am I to doubt Harvard researchers who are saying that long after we go to sleep, our brains "continue to process memories..."? I can't comprehend the Theory of Relativity; taking a nap, I get.

If anything, I am a student of history, and the subject tells me that some of our greatest leaders and thinkers were also nappers. Margaret Thatcher was a napper; so was Albert Einstein, who supposedly napped with a pencil in his hand. When the pencil dropped to the floor, he jostled himself awake, ready to tackle other dimensions. It was said that Thomas Edison never really slept at night at all, surviving instead on a series of catnaps throughout the day; no one ever complained about his productivity. Ronald Reagan napped well before he got into the untimely habit of dropping off during Cabinet meetings, and fellow presidents Franklin Roosevelt and John Kennedy were also known to catch a few minutes of shut-eye during the workday. Bill Clinton says he naps; I'll take his word for it.

Winston Churchill slept often during the day; he was known to do paperwork, write, even paint in his bed, and he did it in his pajamas so that when he felt a nap coming on, he'd be dressed for the occasion. Florence Nightingale took frequent naps too; so did Napoleon, and the story goes that when two assassins tried to get to Harry Truman while he lived in the Blair House (the White House was being renovated), he was still in his underwear after the commotion woke him from his nap.

The truth is, napping has a bad reputation, but that may very well be changing now. From Dagwood Bumstead, who is often found on his couch by that pest of a neighbor, Elmo, to "Seinfeld's" George Costanza, who went to great lengths and expense in one episode to have his work desk built with a hidden bunk installed, the general impression of napping is that it is for the lazy and uninspired. I beg to differ. Bob Hope was a napper, and he lived to be 100; Johannes Brahms literally slept at his piano and said that he dreamed of tunes he would later write down. Who, then, could deprive this poor writer a nap before he sat down at his keyboard to write a few paragraphs?

I already have a documented personal history of napping. My mom used to remind me that I napped as a kid with our old gray cat, Tom, and that I used to sleep near the blowing heat of our furnace's registers. Noticing that I was a bit too quiet, she'd eventually investigate, only to find us, basking together in the warmth that only fuel oil could provide, a tacky old green and pink cotton blanket pulled up to our chins.

It's a fact that many companies these days — Google and Nike being two of them — often provide their workers places to nap during the work day, primarily to hone their creative blades. I saw a television program last year that showed Google's napping areas, complete with futuristic sleeping "pods" that offered ambient sound, temperature controls, soothing colors, even aromatherapy. I have put in suggestions for such a place where I work, but my administrators haven't gotten back with me yet.

According to an article in "Bloomberg Businessweek" from the summer of 2010, writer Jasha Hoffman says that short naps have been shown to "improve alertness, memory, motor skills, decision-making, and mood." I don't know about you, but I sure would be in a better mood if I got to take a nap at work every day about 1 p.m. In my opinion, pre-schoolers have it right: get me on a mat on the floor some afternoon, and I'd be out like a light — no crackers or milk required.

I have had bouts with insomnia over the years; it is my understanding that about 30 percent of all Americans struggle with it from time to time. Although I sleep better now than I did for much of the last decade, I am known to sometimes be in bed by 11 p.m., only to be awake by 1 a.m., spending the next four hours or so staring at the illuminated dial of my watch through bloodshot eyes and enviously listening to the measured breathing of a wife who recharges her batteries without moving a muscle all night long.

I don't care whether it is Stage 2 sleep, short-wave sleep, or REM (rapid eye movement), I need at least 40 winks (an idiom that has a disputed origin), or I get a bit crabby. Happily, the nap I took that late afternoon must have done the trick. I awoke to grade papers and eat supper and act like a decent human being the rest of the evening.

This afternoon, after work, my wife and I walked a while at school; then I came home to work a bit in the yard, and bag trash, and fill our bird feeders, and repair a little wind-blown siding on the house, and, yes, to write this story.

No nap was needed, but it's always nice to know that I have the hang of it now.

Mike Lunsford

Taking 'the road less traveled'
in this illogical life
February 20, 2012

If you can still recall reading the poetry of Robert Frost in your high school English class years ago, I imagine that you can conjure up a line or two from his "The Road Not Taken." In its few simple verses, Frost remembers a time when he faced a choice, that of walking a path in the woods that had been well-trod and worn, or heading down another more overgrown route that "wanted wear."

I teach that poem, and it won't be long before I grab a well-thumbed copy of Frost off my bookshelf and introduce the old boy to my current classes. But I can still recall a student of mine years ago who argued that the poet's choice wasn't really very smart. In fact, it was illogical. Who knew what lay down the untraveled road, he said. If it were worn, wouldn't he know that many others had already taken it? Wasn't the used path easier, perhaps faster? Couldn't he have just saved himself some time?

By the way, his logic was sound, his argument sensible, but I couldn't agree with it, even though I was grateful I had a student who actually wanted to speak to and challenge his teacher a bit. Frost didn't agree with it either; he said that taking the tougher path had "made all the difference."

There is much conjecture as to what Frost meant: a "difference" in what? I need to tell you that I began thinking about Frost and that poem and that conversation not long after speaking to Jayne Virostko, another former student of mine. A school administrator now, she wants me to speak at her academic excellence banquet this spring. I've been wondering ever since about what my topic would be, and I believe that cranky old farmer turned teacher turned poet (Frost, not Jayne) has given me an answer.

Frost was telling us something that most people with a few years behind them already know: If we want to follow a specific plan, and never waiver from it, if we have inflexible schedules and timetables for how our lives are supposed to pan out, then we might as well not live at all.

Like Frost, each of us has strayed down our fair share of unused and weedy paths; we've made more than enough illogical and puzzling choices, too. But, in the long run, those decisions have made a "difference" in our lives — perhaps "the" difference.

I can't help but recall Benjamin Braddock's dilemma in the classic film, "The Graduate." He didn't know what he wanted to do with his life after he had graduated college, and despite advice to go into "plastics" and have a safe future, well, he makes some rather illogical, very human choices. So do I tell these students to always play it safe, to always walk the well-worn path?

I just read a story about a 31-year-old Englishman named Alan Lock, who walked the entire breadth of Antarctica, from coast to coast — some 560 miles — because, as he said, "There are a lot of things I can still do." As if the feat wasn't enough in itself, Lock is nearly blind;

he's lost most of his sight to macular degeneration.

I met a man last year named Byron Pitts, who as a young boy knew that his mother, who was trying to raise him alone in a tough neighborhood in Baltimore, had been told that he was too "retarded" to keep in school. In time, he entered college, conquered a terrible stuttering problem, and now is chief correspondent for CBS' "60 Minutes." His book, "Stepping Out On Nothing," details his illogical, wonderful life.

Then, there is the story of Peter Larson, a 17-year-old high school student from Plymouth, Minn., who just spent his 12th straight year sleeping in a cardboard box from Nov. 12 to Dec. 31, all to inspire others to pledge money to the homeless in his community. So far, he has raised $400,000 and has done so by staying in that box on nights when the temperature has fallen to as low as minus 20 degrees. Larson has said, "...in my heart, I know I'm helping other people."

Twenty-two-year-old U.S. Marine Tyler Southern lost both legs and an arm in an explosion of an IED while serving in Afghanistan in May 2010. He eventually walked his bride down the aisle on his prosthetic legs and re-enlisted in the Marines Corps, yet he faces at least another year-and-a-half of physical therapy. Claiming that he was a lucky man, Southern recently said, "I've got the world at my prosthetic feet."

Every day, we hear about and meet people who have lived those kinds of illogical, improbable lives, folks whose best-laid plans got changed along the way.

Such is the case of Jimmy Doolittle, the World War II bomber commander who led critical raids against Tokyo in April 1942, not long after America was nearly crippled by Japan's attack on Pearl Harbor. Doolittle and his men knew that the odds were against their planes even making it to Japan before being shot down, let alone dropping their bombs and escaping into China. They knew that in all probability they would either run out of fuel and crash or parachute into enemy territory and be captured. But not a single crewman backed out when told of the long odds. They all made wonderfully illogical decisions, and our country was the better for it.

By the way, Doolittle survived the war. He lived a long life and was married to his wife for 71 years. When his granddaughter asked him if he'd ever wished he could live his life over, he supposedly said, "No, I could never be so lucky, again."

He led an illogical, magical life. We should all be so lucky.

Feeding time at the homestead draws a host of new guests
March 5, 2012

I stepped outside into the warmth of an unusually mild early March morning last week to do what I always do just before I grab my briefcase and book bag and lunch bag and head off to work. It's nearly always dark when I leave, even as the sun gets up earlier and earlier in the late winter, so I often go about the business of feeding our cats with porch lights on and a flashlight in hand.

It has been an unwritten agreement between my wife and me that I feed our outdoor felines in the mornings as she tackles her make-up and breakfast rituals. She, on the other hand, has evening duty, most often heading out to the barn or back porch by the time I have my nose stuffed in a book or a blanket pulled up to my chin.

This winter, our cat food consumption has skyrocketed — we have considered investing heavily in Purina stock — and it's taken no more than a few minutes with our noses pressed to our backdoor glass to figure out why: Our cats are having friends over for dinner.

Certainly, our big, old orange tabby cat, Max, is one of the culinary culprits. Normally slim in the summer, Max has swelled to Ralph Kramden-like proportions this winter as age and a general lack of interest in exercise have caught up to him. He tends to eat in increments — a morsel here, a morsel there — but by the end of the day, he has taken in some serious calories. He apparently thinks birds are now beyond his pudgy grasp, and I haven't seen him with a mouse or shrew in his mouth for several years. Some brain activity must pulse behind that dim-witted look of his, for he's always around come feeding time.

Max's meal mate, Lilly, is a rough-looking little survivor. She was dumped out of a car here some years ago and decided that my porch looked more inviting than most.

She is tiny and shy, and she squeaks rather than meows. Lilly doesn't miss many meals, either, but she wasn't eating the epic proportions that we were dispensing. Joanie and I decided surveillance was necessary...

We always knew we had a possum that raided our cat food bowls. We would flick on the light and open our back door in the process of heading to the compost pile or trash can or cabin, and there he'd be, his sardonic grin and greasy tail all part of a generally disgusting package of mismatched parts and picket fence teeth. On most nights, he'd run for the woods or under our deck, but he became more and more brazen as the months went by. I went to scooting him off the deck with a broom. "You'll take it, and like it," I once told him as I did my best impression of private eye Sam Spade. But now, Mr. Possum has a buddy, and if they aren't scavenging for scraps over the hill, they are ambling by the cat dishes to see what's left over.

The rules changed for real a month or so ago, when Joanie headed out the door with some apple peelings and discovered not the white-and-black Lilly eating, but a skunk that was in mid-meal — Joanie even reached out for a quick pat without thinking. Like his café mates, the possums, he high-tailed it off the deck, too, at first.

A few nights later, as Joanie went outside to retrieve the bowl to prevent the raids, Mr. LePew was already at the table, and instead of running, he promptly raised his tail and held his ground. It was Joanie who decided to retreat. Ever more cautious, we decided to announce ourselves to whatever might be chowing down at the cat bowls, clomping our feet and thumping the door before heading through it. A few whiffs of the skunk's cologne made us more wary of what might be munching in the dark, and we'd had raccoons dining in as well.

So, out to the barn our cat dishes went, and instead of us walking out the back door at feeding time, we go out a garage door, head across our basketball court, and dump our food and water in bowls we keep under the barn roof's overhang. I did that just a few weeks ago and found, not the skunk, but a big, gray tomcat that has never bothered to register at our hotel either. He was helping himself to a meal while Max, that generous dim bulb of a host, sat not four feet away and watched him. The new cat has even taken to sleeping in Max's bed, which I would certainly consider an insult, but Max apparently doesn't care about that either. We've grown accustomed to seeing "Thomas" in the barn now, and I imagine he'll be rubbing against our legs in a month or two.

If I didn't know better, I'd swear there's a neon "Eat Here" sign near my place. I pulled in the drive early last week and surprised a flock of starlings as they were dining on our cat food, too. There were enough of them to make Alfred Hitchcock proud, and each bird took advantage of the spilled pieces from a wind-blown plate to snarf a morsel before taking off for the trees.

The piece de resistance, however, came later in the week. Making my way to the barn and the cubbyhole of a tool shop I have there, I saw hoof prints in my driveway. I immediately suspected that my neighbor's horses had been out; for some reason they enjoy grazing in my yard. I'm not miffed about the trespassing at all. Just a month or so ago, my son came by just in time to see a horse wandering around behind our barn, and one of our cats, Nelson, was playfully batting at its nose as it snapped off grass without a care in the world...

But, as it turns out, these hoof prints were not from a horse. I saw my neighbor/English student, and rider of horses, Melissa Manley, at school a few days later, and I asked her if her horses had been loose again. She said no, but her mules — Salmon and Angie — had been, and she was sorry they had run amok in my yard.

I told her I didn't mind; the more the merrier, but I did have indisputable proof — a hoof print smashed into an aluminum pie plate we used as a cat dish — that at least one of them had helped him or herself to our cat food.

As long as they aren't skunks, they're welcome to it.

———

Remembering a Lefty Frizzell-kind of Christmas
December 24, 2012

My brother and sister and I sat around a Thanksgiving dinner table a month ago, shifting in our seats just enough to make our yet-to-be digested turkey sit a little more easily, and, as we often do when we get together, we reminisced about our childhoods for a while. What, I asked, was your favorite childhood Christmas gift?

The question had been prompted by a haphazardly taken snapshot I discovered a few weeks earlier of my brother and sister as they ransacked their gifts on our uncomfortably cold front porch, the site of our Christmas tree in all its bubble-lit and glass-bulbed splendor years and years ago. I can still feel the chill of the porch's tile coming through the insulated feet of my flannel, trap-doored pajamas, still smell the scent of pine when we opened the doors to that magical place as kids on Christmas morning.

The photo was taken before I could walk, I'm sure, so I am not in it, and typically, the panes of the windows of the porch were coated with a glaze of ice. My brother has his back to the camera; my sister is blurred and too close to the lens, her face a glaring flash of nostrils and teeth. But despite my mom's poor work with the Kodak, the picture still brought back a flood of memories, right down to the strands of gaudy tinsel that limply hung from the tree's scrawny limbs.

I already knew what gift I would enter into the discussion, but since I have been agonizingly slow in writing an oft-promised book about such things, I figured I might uncover a story or two for later use if I asked them while I had the chance. As it turned out, I was too surprised, and too pleased with their answers to wait on the book, and so, on this Christmas Eve, I wanted to share.

My brother, John, surprised me with his answer. He is nearly six years older than I am, and he remembered, more realistically, I suppose, what Christmases from those early days were like for us. He can clearly remember when our family desperately struggled financially, when my dad, despite working on construction jobs in such exotic locales (well, to me they were exotic) as Labrador and Washington and Missouri, we barely made ends meet.

One winter, while Dad was away, we were not going to have a Christmas tree at all, and Mom, in hopes she could afford a small one, drove into North Terre Haute just a few days before Christmas, hoping to find one cheap enough to bring home. The salesman at the lot, far from looking prosperous himself, must have sensed how badly Mom wanted a tree, and despite her trying to cram a few crumpled bills into his hands, he refused to be paid for the one he gave to us. With that story in mind, John simply said, "Christmas was always pretty tough on Mom."

As it turned out, despite our "slim" Christmases, my dad supplied John's greatest gift. It was a battleship-sized stereo record player that he'd won on a tavern tip-board near Christmas in 1964, and the sheer novelty of it must have captivated my brother. A rather eclectic collection of records came with the stereo — a huge walnut-encased slab of furniture that matched nothing we had in the house — and for the next few years, we all listened to Lefty Frizzell as he pined for Saginaw, Mich., George Hamilton IV as he longed for Abilene — it was the "prettiest town he'd ever seen" — and Johnny Horton belting it out about the Battle of New Orleans. I think a little Chet Atkins and Elvis Presley, and inexplicably, the soundtrack to "Exodus" were in the mix, too.

My sister didn't hesitate with her story, either. She said that as Christmas neared, and it may have been in the very same year dad brought the stereo home, my mom had grown increasingly nervous when the topic of gifts had come up, and that as the big day approached she had told my sister that her present might not be brought by Santa on Christmas Eve, that it may come a few days later. As it turned out, Sis eventually discovered that Mom had ordered her a pair of dolls, a "Tiny and Big Thumbelina" set by Ideal, both of which, if I recall correctly, had huge, growth-like knobs in the small of their backs, that, when turned, made their arms and legs robotically move. The dolls also looked as if it they had badly botched heads of hair plugs, but, of course, that's the way dolls' scalps looked in those days.

Mom had ordered the dolls from the Spiegel's catalog, and day after day, she waited for them, knowing they were what Sis wanted more than anything else. She called the store every day; she even called Walt Williams, our kindly old mailman (I used to wait for him every summer day on our front hillside just to have someone to talk to) who told her that if the dolls came, he'd bring them to the house, even on Christmas Eve if necessary. As it turned out, they didn't come for Christmas, but when Walt brought them to the house a week or so later, Mom went ahead and wrapped them. My sister still remembers the red corduroy dresses the dolls wore, and said, "I was disappointed about not getting them on Christmas morning, but not traumatized. We didn't get much for Christmas, so it was still exciting when I did finally get them."

My favorite gift is one that will play a big role in that yet-to-be-finished book, if I ever get it written. It was a plastic "Fort Apache" play set, resplendent with its plastic stockade fence, plastic blockhouses, plastic totem pole, and plastic teepee. Of course, plastic cowboys and Indians and Calvary soldiers accompanied the set, and I played with it so often, and so loudly, that both my brother and sister begged my mom to make me play without the accompanying sound effects. That proved impossible, so they either had to live with hearing the bloodcurdling screams of Indian raiding parties, the blares of Army bugles, and the gunfire of frontier battle action, or go listen to Lefty Frizzell ...

I don't think I ever noticed that our Christmases

were low-budget affairs in those days. And even though I know I can never go back to that ice box of a porch and that Charlie Brown pine tree, except in my memories, I don't think I will ever be nearly as rich.

On this day above all,
'Peace on earth, good will to men'
December 25, 2012

More than a year after his wife's death, the great American poet, Henry Wadsworth Longfellow, wrote in his diary on Christmas Day. "'A merry Christmas' say the children, but that is no more for me. Perhaps someday God will grant me peace."

It is an often-told story. Longfellow, who had endured the death of his first wife in 1832, had lost his second, Frances, in 1861 to a tragic fire, and the grieving widower was in despair. He was a man who had come to know sorrow and loneliness and anger.

In the wake of what has happened in Newtown, through the pall that has been cast over us this Christmas by the murderous evil that manifested itself there, something can be learned from Longfellow and how he turned his grief and sorrow toward faith and understanding. He never got over Fanny's death. That is evident in his sonnet, "A Cross of Snow," written in 1879, but he did understand that hope could emerge from heartache, and, for us, that may be the only real lesson we can take from what has transpired in Connecticut these past few weeks.

In the spring of 1861, Longfellow and Fanny, and their five children, were living happy lives. He was America's most established and popular poet, known for his depictions of Paul Revere, the wreck of the good ship Hesperus, Miles Standish's courtship, and so many others. He was among the nation's most outspoken opponents of slavery, and he and his wife lived in a beautiful and already historic home (Craigie House had been General Washington's Revolutionary War headquarters for a while), given to the couple by Fanny's father. Life in that house near the Charles River in Cambridge was safe and secure, despite it being the opening months of the Civil War.

But on July 9, while sealing some of 7-year-old daughter Edith's newly clipped curls in wax, Fanny's dress caught fire. Despite her husband's attempts to put out the flames, she was horribly burned and died the next day. Longfellow carried the scars, both emotionally and physically, the rest of his life.

It would be months before he could even speak of Fanny's death. In a letter to his brother, Longfellow wrote, "And now, of what we both are thinking I can write no word. God's will be done." To a visitor at Craigie House, who told Longfellow that he hoped the poet would "be able to bear his cross," the poet replied, "Bear the cross, yes, but what if one is stretched upon it?" On the first Christmas after Fanny's death, Longfellow wrote in his diary, "How inexpressibly sad are all holidays... I can make no record of these days. Better leave them wrapped in silence."

Longfellow's grief was later compounded when his oldest son, Charles, left home to join the Union Army without his father's permission. On March 14, 1863, the poet received a letter from Charley, who wrote, "I have tried hard to resist the temptation of going without your leave, but I cannot any longer ... I feel it to be my first duty to do what I can for my country, and I would willingly lay down my life for it if it would be of any good."

That November, Longfellow received word that his boy had been wounded at the Battle of New Hope Church in Virginia. He and another son, Erny, traveled to Washington to bring Charles home and care for him. Longfellow expected his son would die, but he didn't.

By Christmas Day, 1863, Longfellow, perhaps inspired by a year in which the Union armies had won stunning victories at Gettysburg and Vicksburg, and his son's recovery, wrote a poem called "Christmas Bells." Two of his stanzas directly referred to the war, yet even while the fighting still raged, and in fact, the slaughter grew worse, it was Longfellow's oft-repeated lines that proved most touching: "Then pealed the bells more loud and deep/ God is not dead; nor doth he sleep!/ The Wrong shall fail,/ The Right prevail,/ With peace on earth, good-will to men!"

In 1872, composer Jean Baptiste Calkin set the poem to music, removing the two verses that referenced the war, and the poem became the beloved hymn, "I Heard the Bells on Christmas Day."

The massive bells of the National Cathedral rang last Friday at 9:30 a.m. They pealed 28 times for the victims in Newtown, and, yes, even for the man who took their lives. They rang all across the country, and they rang in the churches of Newtown, as well. In ages past, the sounds of bells were used to call those of faith to pray for the departed dead, and so they should still be reminders for us to do the same. But like Longfellow's words, they can also be heard as the peals of hope.

Years later, Longfellow wrote "The Bells of San Blas," which was published a few months after his death in 1882. Those words are fitting for us, too. He wrote: "The world rolls into light / It is daybreak everywhere."

On the simple joys of watching it snow...
January 7, 2013

It began to snow about 20 minutes ago, as I write this, light, wind-driven flakes that fall silently into my woods as I watch from a window. It wasn't unexpected, for the weather man has been telling us for a few days that we should be looking for another inch or two by the New Year. He needn't have bothered, for when I pulled on my boots this morning and headed out to our birdfeeder with a coffee can of sunflower seeds and an ear of shell corn in my hands, I could smell the newness of it coming in the air. All I had to do was be patient.

A few years ago, I wrote a story about the satisfaction I felt in having my walks and back deck clear of the frequent snows we had been getting all winter. It seemed as though every other day brought a solid promise of at least a dusting — or more — and I spent those mostly bleak, gray months scraping and heaving it away from our doors, and re-plowing a pathway to the barn.

But, since I needed the solitude and the exercise, I grumbled little, and even began to enjoy my daily waltz with a snow shovel.

It is just a feeling — call it "shoveler's intuition," if you will — that this winter is to be similar. An inch here, and two inches there, and I will find myself in late February finally saying, "I've had enough." But, for now anyway, I am enjoying myself, as are the birds on my place, for they know I am much more diligent about slopping their hash a few more times a day when snow is in the forecast.

I should have guessed days ago that this year's snow will be heavier than last year's, but not because I diligently read the "Old Farmer's Almanac" or delight in watching the wooliness of worms or the height of hornet's nests. One hint came a few weeks ago as I walked to the house after a trip to the mailbox. Thumbing through the recycling that has become my mail, a huge snowflake fell on the back of my black-gloved hand. It was the most perfect flake I think I have ever seen, and within minutes of its demise in the warmth of the house, I was searching the Internet in hope of finding just what its pattern was called.

That job didn't prove too difficult, particularly since I found a fascinating webpage put together by Dr. Ken Libbrecht, the chairman of the physics department at the California Institute of Technology. According to the good doctor, who prefers to refer to a chart that identifies 35 basic types of snowflakes, there may be upward of 80 different kinds of snow crystals. My companion flake was a "stellar dendrite," and Libbrecht says they are "clearly the most popular snow crystal type, seen in holiday decorations everywhere. You can see these crystals for yourself quite well with just a simple magnifier." Libbrecht also says, "'dendritic' means 'tree-like,' so stellar dendrites are plate-like snow crystals that have branches and sidebranches. These are fairly large crystals, typically 2-4 mm [millimeters] in diameter, easily seen with the naked eye."

In fact, I'm not sure that my snowflake wasn't a "fernlike stellar dendrite," formed when even more sidebranches develop. Libbrecht says, "These are the largest snow crystals, often falling to earth with diameters of 5 mm or more. In spite of their large size, these are single crystals of ice — the water molecules are lined up from one end to the other."

I have always been interested in the science of nature; I reveled in a childhood of telescopes and microscopes and leaf collections. But I enjoyed the snowflake for more aesthetic reasons than the science of it;

it is the same reason why I still search the night sky for meteors, why I watch sunlight play on the water of a lake, why I still pick up rocks and fossils and lug them home to sit on a window sill. I know, for instance, that snowflakes are given birth by clouds that cruise at high elevations, and that little bits of grit can even act as cores for the infant flakes. I know that snowflakes begin as tiny droplets of condensation, and that as more and more water vapor condenses onto their surface, they grow, perhaps, eventually into six-sided crystals that become so heavy that they fall out of the clouds. Dr. Libbrecht certainly knows that, too, but I was willing to wager that even he finds snowflakes more beautiful than merely something to study, so I wrote him to find out.

"I find that studying snowflakes has both a scientific side and an artistic side, and I enjoy both," Libbrecht wrote in his response. "The scientific side is figuring out the molecular dynamics of how crystals grow, which is both fascinating and potentially useful. The artistic side arises just because the crystals are quite beautiful."

In one passage Libbrecht includes on his webpage, he writes: "...it's even a bit amazing, when you stop to ponder it — the whole complex, beautiful, symmetrical structure of a snow crystal simply arises spontaneously, quite literally out of thin air, as it tumbles through the clouds."

Despite their science, I really care most that those

flakes fall onto my gloved hands, and onto the branches of my trees. I enjoy watching them, driven along by a west wind as they accumulate on my eaves and fence posts and woven wire and cabin railing. They even cling to the whiskers of my old cat, Max, who despite having warmer quarters in the barn and its straw, illogically sleeps on the deck near a back corner of our house in a snowfall that will eventually render him a muted orange lump until he wakes himself.

These observations remind me of a poem by Kate DiCamillo called "Snow, Aldo." In it, the poet observes an old man who, while walking his dog in a park, laughs and holds his face upward toward the falling snow. "Snow, Aldo," the old man says. "Snow," he repeats, and the dog wags its tail. The poem is a reminder for me about the simple joys of watching it snow, of the shear wonder of it.

The snow is coming down harder now. It is slowly, but surely filling in the bootprints I made this morning as I brought an armload of fireplace wood to my backdoor. I left my snow shovel leaning against my cabin, and already a ridge of new snowfall has accumulated on its handle. It is growing colder, and the volume of the world's sounds is being turned down as the big, fat flakes continue to fall.

The weatherman says it may snow a bit again this weekend, although he's not expecting much. I have my shovel ready, just in case.

———

Cheerful green of wheat fights winter blahs

January 21, 2013

There is a light drizzle of freezing rain tapping at the door of my cabin today. It is little more than a week before the words I am writing are due to appear on your breakfast table or work desk with your morning coffee and scrambled eggs. But I write when I can, and today, despite a full schedule of televised football games, and the stacks of ungraded papers in my briefcase, and a good book lying open on my nightstand, I am clacking away on a keyboard to the whir of a heater and the steady drip of my gutters.

I am considering a careful walk to my truck in a few minutes. I want to pull it under the overhang of a rusting tin roof so I won't be scraping an ice-glazed windshield tomorrow morning in the dark. Incongruous to the past few days' worth of unseasonably warm January days, the icy rain makes me want to pull on a thicker sweatshirt, hunker down and wait for spring, but I was reminded again just this morning that a little bit of green can go a long way in the winter months to encourage a bud of optimism. Looking at the long-term forecast and its oncoming freight train of frigid arctic air, I may need a bit of encouragement...

Just across the road from my place, a farmer friend has planted acres and acres of winter wheat, and even before it disappeared beneath a blanket of snow a few weeks ago, it was as green as a golf course fairway. I love wheat fields, particularly in the wintertime, for they are cheerful reminders that spring and lawn mowers and leafy trees are never far away. I thought those very thoughts as I retrieved my morning paper today, standing near my mailbox to look over the field as it was raked by a wet northwesterly wind.

Years ago, I asked Artie Yeargin, who farms the rolling clay of the farmland to the west of us, if he'd consider planting a little wheat, and so, two falls ago, he did just that. I have always liked to watch wheat blow in the spring wind, enjoy it even as it lies dormant through the winter. By late June or early July — earlier last year since we had precious little moisture — winter wheat is ready for harvest. By then, it is a uniform blanket of reedy gold stalks, their fat heads rocking in the breeze like metronomes.

I don't know if Artie planted the wheat just to get me to be quiet or not. I had always heard that wheat can be a tenuous crop to grow, for much can go wrong. Timing, of course, is important, and it needs plenty of nitrogen, and it is susceptible to a host of pests and diseases. But, I have also heard there is money to be made from it, that one of its benefits is that wheat fields can be doubled-cropped with soybeans, and, of course, there is straw to be harvested as well.

I have no idea of his reasoning, but Artie planted even more wheat this fall, and I couldn't be happier, for on gray days such as this, there is that ever-present green just across the road.

Centuries ago, long before we could walk down grocery store aisles and grab loaves of bread and packages of muffins and boxes of cereal from the racks and shelves, wheat was eaten like I eat popcorn: by the handful. People gathered the seeds, rubbed the husks together and chewed what was left in their palms. Wheat is actually a grass, originating near the "Cradle of Civilization," in what is now modern-day Iraq. That's a long way and ages from being today's buttered toast or bowl of "Wheaties."

According to the Wheat Foods Council, wheat was first cultivated in the United States just a year or so after the Revolution began, primarily as a "hobby crop." Now, it's grown in 42 states, and more than 75 percent of all American grain products involve wheat flour in one way or another. The latest statistics I found determined that Kansas grows more wheat than any other state, although North Dakota isn't very far behind. A single acre of Kansas farmland can produce enough bread to feed more than 9,000 people for a day, and one estimate says that the entire state grows enough wheat in a year to feed every human being on the planet for two whole weeks (or keep my son in cereal for a month).

Of course, farming is actually science, and I am interested as to how wheat stays green at a time when so many other plants, including many of my "evergreens," turn anemic and brown. After being planted in mid to late fall, winter wheat (scientific name *Triticum aestivum*) seedlings begin a process called "cold acclimation." The seedlings pop their heads through the soil when the temperature drops below 50 degrees or so, and as it absorbs light, wheat produces considerable quantities of carbon, storing it in its crown. The combination of the colder air and the carbon helps the plants store energy for the spring thaws. Ironically, wheat needs cold weather to be able to flower.

I have said it before about things that require more brains than I have to understand: The science of the natural world interests me, but I appreciate its beauty more, and for that field of wheat across the road, I am thankful, not only for the bread it will produce, but for the mood it puts me in. I don't know exactly what variety of the six main kinds of wheat Artie has planted, and I don't much care since gluten and I are good friends, and pasta is one of my best buddies.

In the early summer, I'll watch the wheat fields turn to gold, and combines will move across them in an early harvest. But, for now, the wheat's green encouragement in this bleak mid-winter gives me what I really need.

Twain's Sawyer helps us yearn for 'wilderness of childhood'
February 4, 2013

"SATURDAY morning was come, and all the summer world was bright and fresh, and brimming with life. There was a song in every heart; and if the heart was young the music issued at the lips. There was cheer in every face and a spring in every step. The locust-trees were in bloom and the fragrance of the blossoms filled the air.

Cardiff Hill, beyond the village and above it, was green with vegetation and it lay just far enough away to seem a Delectable Land, dreamy, reposeful, and inviting."
Mark Twain's "The Adventures of Tom Sawyer"

My cousin, Roger, stopped in one day last summer for a glass of tea and a little conversation. Rog has lived an hour's drive away for years, and now, and besides summer reunions, I don't see him nearly often enough. He's a good man who has raised a good family, and he owns a healthy sense of appreciation for not only the life he has now, but also the lives we had years ago as kids.

We talked the afternoon away that day, ignoring our work, but adding considerably to the stockpile of memories I plan to share with readers in a book that's still only a quarter of the way done. But what he said as he walked out the door to head home stayed with me the most, primarily because it was so true: "We were really lucky to grow up where we did," he said.

We (that includes his brother and sister, and my brother and sister) didn't lead lives of privilege and luxury. We most certainly lived with grandparents and parents who loved and looked after us, but they also encouraged us to develop a spirit of adventure and use our imaginations as we explored the woods and creeks that made up our back yards. That's not to say that we were never bored, but I honestly can't recall being in that condition very often; there was just too much to do.

I had that thought in mind last fall as I re-read

Mark Twain's "The Adventures of Tom Sawyer" for the first time in years. Through Sawyer, Twain undoubtedly relived a bit of his own childhood, one that wasn't easy, nor often very romantic. He was working by the time he was 12, and had already lost his father and two siblings by then.

Roger was no Huck Finn — although he and my brother, John, did attempt some rather harrowing feats, most of which flew in the face of the laws of gravity — and I was certainly no Tom. There was no river rafting, no school skipping, no life-threatening escapades in graveyards and caves and courtrooms. But, we practically lived outdoors in those days, blessed, I suppose, by televisions that were lucky to pull in three fuzzy stations, and a wooded and watered terrain that just begged for grape vine swinging and wading and tree climbing. My parents did their parts by encouraging the camping and crawdad catching and dirt clod throwing.

That may not be the case nearly as much anymore, and even though children now are growing up in a different world than the one that helped raise Roger and me, activity and exploration and self-developed spirits of inquiry and adventure, as Huck and Tom most certainly had, seem to be less and less prevalent. Luckily, we didn't experience our childhoods like Huck, whose mother had died and who faced the abuse of an alcoholic father. Readers never really learn why and how Tom was orphaned, so at least part of his and Huck's stories serve as reminders to us that not all children can experience idyllic, play-filled childhoods. But, despite their troubles, Tom and Huck prevail, and certainly their spirits of adventure helped them do it.

Most of the statistics I found about childhood play these days are dated, but it's apparent that folks have been concerned about our kids' inactivity for years. One study of childcare providers in the Cincinnati area, as reported by author Lenore Skenazy, suggested that children of pre-school age were spending only 2 to 3 percent of their day in "vigorous activity." Skenazy says: "Children spending 97 percent of their day not running around? It's like a desk job, except with cookie time ... it's bad. Bad for their bodies, their brains, their blubber."

Author Michael Chabon wrote a fascinating essay on the subject for the "New York Review of Books" in 2009 (I read it in "Smithsonian Magazine") called "The Wilderness of Childhood." He said, "People read stories of adventure — and write them — because they have themselves been adventurers. Childhood is, or has been, or ought to be, the great original adventure, a tale of privation, courage, constant vigilance, danger, and sometimes calamity."

Of course, much of that "calamity" is experienced through our imaginations, the powerful voices in our heads and hearts, that can't be duplicated on a computer monitor or television screen or phone. Twain's childhood wilderness was Hannibal, Chabon's, a copse of woodland on the edge of a small town in Maryland. For Roger and me, it was the shallow water of Spring Creek to the west, the sandy ridges of Old Man Stahl's fields to the east, Lyman Pendergast's wooded field road to the south, and the ancient beech tree atop my uncle's hill to the north. It was a world just big enough to get lost in one afternoon at a time.

Twain's romantic vision of the Mississippi, of Jackson's Island, of Cardiff Hill, and McDougal's Cave are universal. We can relive or reinvent our own "Wilderness of Childhood" through Tom Sawyer's adventures. We might even be inspired to help our children explore their own.

The 'lovely gift' of a beech tree ...
February 18, 2013

This is not the season that I usually write of trees, for besides a few pin oaks that hang on to the most stubborn of leaves, my woods stand bare and dormant and cold right now. My trees are patiently awaiting the green of spring that I feel, for some reason, is to arrive a little earlier this year than is usual.

I have always believed that as a writer, I have to strike while the iron is hot, and so when I unearthed an article on the American beech tree as I excavated a messy desktop one morning last week, I knew then and there that I wanted to write about them.

Despite having a growing queue of writing ideas at the moment, the smooth, gray bark of the trees remained foremost in my mind, and so, beeches it shall be, and my thanks to Michael Homoya, the plant ecologist who wrote the piece, for the reminder.

There are just a few beech trees in my woods, but on my home ground, just three or four miles and a few decades south of here, I came to know them well. We had a gorgeous beech just a few feet from our front door, and across the road sat a huge old majestic specimen that marked the northernmost edge of my world. I suppose, however, that a beech that stood just off my grandfather's driveway led me to love them the way I do. I have written of that particular tree before, for my dad and my grandfather wanted it cut down for years, and eventually, over my protest, they got the job done. As much as I loved them both, their destructive persistence still irks me a bit most of a lifetime later.

Although I own a half-dozen handbooks on trees, Homoya's article in the latest edition of "Outdoor Indiana" serves as both reference book and memoir. He wrote, "As monarchs of the forest, the American beech displays a presence that few other species can match."

Amen to that, for beeches often grow to reach 80 feet or more in height, and produce crowns that spread even wider. According to a big tree registry I sometimes thumb through, the biggest beech tree in Indiana (found in Vanderburgh County) is 91 feet tall. I am not exaggerating when I say that several of the beeches I recall from home were nearly as gigantic. It is known that some beeches live for more than 400 years, and according to Homoya, they, along with the American chestnut, belong to the same plant family — *Fagaceae* — as do oaks. They are slow-growing trees, and although they can prosper just about anywhere, beeches tend to prefer "deep ravines, north-facing slopes, and better-drained portions of flatwoods." Nearly every beech tree I can remember from my childhood roamings grew on hillsides, as do the few I have in my woods now, for all I have are hillsides on my property.

Beechwood is harvested commercially. It is hard and tightly grained, and it is often used in flooring and crates and even tool handles and artwork. It makes excellent charcoal, and the oil from beechnuts was once used in oil lamps. In fact, our ancestors, who seemed to use about anything and everything at their disposal as either medicines or meals (I once heard that pioneers ate roasted mice as a way to ward off illness), did so with everything the beech tree had to offer. They ate beechnuts raw, even cooked them and ground them into a sort of flour. Boiled beech leaves produced a poultice often used on everything from poison ivy to frostbite.

According to Homoya, beech trees are important for the life of a forest. Most of the oldest become hollow in their declining years. These "cavities" supply shelter to several species of birds, and flying squirrels are known to favor them as homes, as well. When the tops of the trees break off, they create natural "chimneys" for chimney swifts that have been unable to settle in more modern digs. Hollow beech trunks near the ground are often nesting spots for turkey vultures.

Of course, I couldn't have known any of those things when I played in and under the beeches we had, but I do stand guilty as charged when Homoya wrote, "A destructive minority of pocket-knife carriers insist on carving up [the] trunks..." My name, crudely and crookedly adorns the beech closest to our old place, something I've been reminded of by the folks who now live there. My grandfather had given me a pocket knife, so naturally I had to try it out. I don't believe I've taken that knife, which I am saving for a grandchild, to more than a sassafras twig since.

Despite the fact that my grandfather was a fierce feller of trees, my Grandmother Blanche loved the beeches near our houses, and she rarely approved of her husband's hastiness with a crosscut saw. She once confided in her diary, just minutes after my grandfather had "trimmed" her lilac bushes a little too aggressively: "I'd like to kick him in the shins." My family lived just a stone's throw from my grandparents' back door, and between us, among the red oaks and tulip poplars and persimmons, stood a wonderful pair of beech trees.

After she died, barely 60, a poem my grandmother wrote was found in her tattered Bible. My sister re-discovered it just a month or two ago and sent it on to me, another reason why, I suppose, I needed to write about beech trees.

She wrote:

I have a big beech tree
Over on the hill
I often climb upon the branches
and sometimes I take a spill.
Then I lie down upon the grass
And look up in the tree
And watch the birds building their nests
A wondrous sight to see.
And then I think how much love
God has for you and me
to make such lovely gifts as a beautiful big beech tree.

Near the end of his piece, Homoya eloquently wrote, "When a tree departs, all the life that depended on it follows suit." To that, I say, "Amen," too.

If handwriting is a window to my soul, I'm glad this is typewritten
March 4, 2013

Somewhere in the mess I call my "archives," I have most of my grade school report cards hidden away. I have kept them under wraps, because I want to be long gone when my children — or grandchildren — unearth them and discover that their self-righteous teacher of a dad was, in fact, a terrible student in his formative years.

Without those damning bits of evidence available, I have been able to convince friends and family that I was on the fast track to being a Rhodes scholar, that I was president of the high school Rocket Club, that I actually discovered absolute zero fooling around on a notepad during grade school recess. But one thing is apparent: I haven't been able to sell anyone the notion that my handwriting has ever been legible.

I did find my sixth-grade card, and there in the gracefully looped cursive of my teacher, Wanda Thomas, was that ever-present C- in handwriting — a gift, I imagine, to help soften the blow for my mother, who was probably already depressed as she glanced through a litany of "unsatisfactories" and Ds. I am happy to say, however, that I did have near-perfect attendance, and I "respected the property of others."

Despite the fact that my handwriting now appears to be the product of a hypertensive lunatic, I truly believe that teaching the formation of printed letters, then cursive writing, is critical to the development of any child, even one like I was. It seemed as though no matter how I held my tongue, I could not make a pencil work the way I wanted it to.

With the advent of the new Common Core standards in Indiana schools, a path, I suspect, on which we shouldn't be trudging, comes the de-emphasis of handwriting in elementary schools in favor of "keyboarding." That decision has created a brushfire of criticism and concern. Indiana University neuroscientist Karen Harman James is one of those worrying. James, who may have been an actual Rocket Club president, is best known for the landmark research she's conducted at IU on the importance of handwriting and the development of children's brains.

"Printing is critical," James told me last week, "because it is a fine motor skill. Fine motor skill acquisition is crucial for many aspects of cognitive development. For brain development, practice printing sets up the reading network that is used later during reading acquisition."

In other words, James says that teaching kids to write by hand, even printing (her jury is still out on cursive), is critical to how children eventually learn to read. What appears to some as being a minor shift from early printing, and perhaps cursive writing, toward keyboarding, may have a major impact on how kids read and learn.

In a piece written for "IU Newsroom" last week, James said, "We have recently shown that when children look at letters, the activity in parts of their brains becomes more like activity seen in literate adult brains, but only after they have had practice printing letters."

Theresa Ortega is not a neuroscientist, but she is a certified handwriting analyst who has spent much of a lifetime fascinated by how our brains and hands work together to form letters. An administrative assistant in Indiana State University's Student Recreation Center, Ortega also runs a private business and has lectured on handwriting analysis for years.

"Handwriting is brainwriting," Ortega says, and like James, she is very concerned about students' brain development as they grasp the digital world through a keyboard instead of with a pencil. Ortega made sure that I understood that handwriting analysis "can't detect chronological age, gender, race, religion, or the future," but it certainly can be revealing.

In a recent interview, Ortega said that she has analyzed hundreds, if not thousands, of young adults (high school and college aged) who told her that they were not taught cursive writing. More troubling to her, however, is "I find a very large group of students who are trending toward introversion, a lack of ability to express emotion, an inability to form relationships, and an inability to think critically and creatively."

Ortega added, "This, of course, is being helped along by the technology that has invaded and permeated our lives... I think we need the connectivity of cursive writing to equalize the force of technology."

Ortega volunteered to analyze my scrawl, a sample of which I donated with two exceptions: first, that she also analyze my wife's handwriting, and second, that she not notify authorities if she were to find some sort of criminal or emotionally unstable tendency in my chicken scratches. I imagined that she'd find Joanie's writing to be that of a humanitarian award winner, while mine would have me placed on an FBI watch list.

After assuring me that most people nervously joke about such things when they give her a handwriting sample, Ortega did, in fact, determine that my wife was very intelligent, seeks compromise, and is "down-to-earth." She said that Joanie could be stubborn (no comment from me here), but that she "likes people to get along and be cooperative." Her analysis was spot on.

As for me, Ortega hit it out of the park, too. She determined that I "liked to read," so my early letter formation must have done its job in helping that part of my brain to develop. She said I am a "quick thinker," but that I may also be "impatient with others who don't think as quickly." She also said I was "self-conscious," "hard" on myself, and that I form what she calls a "Go to hell K." That is, when I'm told I can't do something, my handwriting suggests that I'm thinking: "...I'm doing it anyway."

Ortega went on to say that Common Core's de-emphasis of handwriting is simply a bad idea. "I think we need to stop these knee-jerk reactions of 'Oh, let's just yank it out because it's antiquated and nobody is gonna use it.' I'm saying that the processes a child's brain goes through to learn it are invaluable to that child's development."

Nellie Neal, my first grade teacher, has been gone a long time, but I hear that my second grade teacher, Miss Casper, who worked very hard to do her best for my handwriting, is still in the area. To them both, I say, "Thank you for helping me learn how to write." Not everyone might think that was such a good idea, though...

Mike Lunsford

-Spring-

"In the spring, I have counted 136 different kinds of
weather inside of 24 hours."   Mark Twain

*A report from the country brings
sense of renewal*

March 19, 2012

Regardless of what the calendar may yet say, spring
has happened. It couldn't have come too soon, and it wasn't
just last week and its windy 70s that have convinced me. I
have been keeping a journal of sorts in my head for a
fortnight now, stashing away reports of birds and buds and
sounds in the crammed cabinets of my mind, all in a file
marked, "The New Season."

Despite the gale-force winds of the early month, my
wife and I have been walking our road in the early
evenings. As I write this, we just braved nearly 3 miles of
gusts, our hair soon looking like a pair of old bird nests
that have come unraveled. In succession, I noted an Eastern
Bluebird, a lonely dandelion, a very green willow tree, a
solitary crocus, a pair of men who stood fishing in short
pants, and a brown-and-white duck that walked to the
pond's edge, upright — like a man in a back brace —
before sliding into the water as smoothly as a john boat.

The wind battered us, but the nice weather keeps
us from walking the halls of our school in the late
afternoons, a habit we have gotten into when it is too cold
or wet to walk outdoors.

We slogged against the breezes, not unlike an old dog that is wary of an outstretched hand, and once I turned to look for traffic just in time for the wind to fill my shirt like a sail and push me into a ditch.

These are good things, almost as pleasing as the frogs I hear through the screened window of my cabin. They are happy to be up from the ooze and out from under their tree bark prison cells, finally into the sun, all calling out loudly for dates in their slimy lonely hearts clubs. They are happiest, it seems to me, in the very early morning when the stars are still out, and at dusk, as if they appreciate the sunset as much as I do.

I went to work in my yard two Saturdays ago. It was a cloudless, sunny and breezy day, so I washed out my coffee cup and tugged on the jeans that I leave by the garage's back door in late fall. I donned a pair of hiking boots and my favorite ball cap, too, and headed outside to do what I could do.

Although I was a bit tired when I came in a few hours later, it felt good to breathe air that had not come to me through a furnace filter, and the warmth of the sun crept through my thin long-sleeved shirt. Had it been a little warmer, I'd have let it get to the pale skin of my arms, for I have grown white in my jackets and sweaters this winter. It didn't take long for me to drop my gloves off at the doorstep; I didn't need them, and I thought a little dirt under my nails wouldn't hurt, either.

I have been able to get outside off and on this

winter, and I have managed to keep the yard policed, plucking the occasional beer can or tree limb or paper napkin up from where the wind has deposited it. But there was much more than that to do, so first, I fired up an old weed trimmer, on which I keep a saw blade, and gave our tall ornamental grasses nice flat-tops. We like to see the frost on the grass all winter, but tiny green shoots of new growth were hankering to get up and at it, so I evened things up and tossed the old brown grass over the back hill.

I raked pile after pile of leaves and twigs, as well. I often thought our lawn looked nice as the winter wiled itself away — I could still see the lines I cut into it with my mower last November — yet it yielded wheelbarrow loads of the brown and brittle trash, mostly blown into the niches of my flower beds and shrubs and rock walls. Our fat barn cat, Max, followed me around the yard like a devoted friend, but never offered to help me at all. He mostly came near my work, then would promptly plop himself into a sunny spot to sleep a while. And for that, he still expects a full food dish.

There were surprises to be found, first in the scraggy potted mums that I needed to empty. All winter long, those pots sat against a fence, the mums in them crunchy and dead. But as I picked up the first pot, I noticed that the plant inside was still alive. In fact, all but 2 of the 10 pots had generous amounts of growth in them, bits of the living among the dead. When the ground warms, they'll go into it, and not without some guilt on my part, for I left them unplanted last fall because I was too faithless to believe they'd make it through the winter anyway. "Hardy" has become a catchword for "Dead by December" to me, but these mums must have come from stouter stock.

After attending the mum revival, I worked on an old trellis that blew over last month and fractured a support. It has been kept together with a few wood screws and a promise for the past few years, but I have it standing up again, ready to do battle with spring rains and summer sun. We'll see if it can go another year.

I have built an impressive pile of twigs and limbs behind my barn, and I am just about ready to set a match to it. I added considerable fuel to the pyre that day, and I re-stacked rock and cleaned my gutters and swept my walks clean. I saw that the buds are budding, the irises are up, the grass is greening, and I even had to pull a few weeds.

Before I walked into the garage, I thought about how fortunate I was to be picking up around the house, rather than picking up what was left of my house, as those in West Liberty and Henryville are doing in the wake of the terrible storms that hit there a few weeks ago. I know that the spring wind is a fickle old gal, and my mind went to that tragedy often. I was gathering up just a few twigs and tired old leaves; there was no grumble or complaint to be found in me on a day when the sun shone, and I was breathing good air into my lungs.

In this report from the country, I am glad to say

that the sassafras is green and the raspberry briars and the honeysuckle have small ruby-colored leaves of new growth on them; I can smell the flowers of the latter in imagined summer breezes already. It felt good to walk around with tools in my hands and a little sweat in my hair, and later that night, I felt lucky to be able to look to the western sky and see the celestial dance that was played by Venus and Jupiter.

It was a day to bend and stretch and think.

'When lilacs last in the dooryard bloom'd...'
April 2, 2013

Had white lace curtains been hanging in the west window of my cabin, I would have had a perfect Wyeth painting to watch last Thursday. A gentle breeze was wafting through my screens, and the sunlight of a warm late March day was fractured by the window sill as it poured onto my legs and feet. I could catch the scent of lilacs as it was carried in by that wind, and it and the subtle melody of the chimes that hang just outside made me as lazy as an old cat.

We have not always had lilacs in our yard, and we have never had them in bloom as early as they are now. For years, I cultivated a lilac bush near the mouth of our driveway, trimming and fertilizing and encouraging it to produce a crop of fragrant blooms, but it never did. There is not enough sunlight in the spot for which I was determined to see that bush prosper, and finally, after years of stubbornly trying to make it do that which it couldn't, I moved a few shoots of it closer to the house, into one of the few sunny spots I have in my yard. We have been rewarded this spring.

My stubbornness was not the only thing at fault, however. I learned just this year that lilacs do not like to grow near black walnut trees, that the latter produce a chemical called "juglone"—known by mad scientists as 5-hydroxy-1,4-naphthalenedion—and flowering shrubs, like lilacs and hydrangeas, don't care for the stuff at all. In fact, they most often do one of two things when they happen to be situated near walnuts: They either die, or renounce their blooms in protest. Since our lilac bush sat within 20 feet or so of not one, but two walnut trees (one of which is now just a stump), it had several reasons to snub us.

A few days ago, as Joanie and I were headed along the road in our walking shoes to see what we could see, we met Julia Hickman and her shiny Buick as they pulled into our neighbor's drive. Birch Bailey, who lives across the fence from us — he was named after his grandfather rather than a tree or a senator — has five huge lilac bushes growing in his yard. It has probably been his blooms that we have been sniffing over our way, since his is a bumper crop this spring. Julia thought she'd snip a few to take home. She passed us a few minutes later in a whirl of dust, her lilac clippings tucked away on her front seat.

The lilac — scientific name *syringa vulgaris* — was first cultivated in Eastern Europe. The name — originally, nilak — is Persian and means "bluish." Our name for the plant is a Spanish variant. Lilacs are part of the olive family, and some can grow as tall as 30 feet. There are two dozen species of shrubs and trees that are called lilacs, and there are perhaps up to a 1,000 varieties of them.

As is most often the case when I begin a commentary on something of which I know practically nothing, I have begun to read a bit about lilacs, and I have been surprised with what I've found. For instance, according to one source, lilacs are edible, although I am not advocating such a thing. Lilacs can be crystallized and candied for cookies, pies and cakes, and they can be added to salads, too. One recipe calls for fresh lilac blossoms to be mixed with honey and yogurt for an "elegant" dessert, and I have heard that lilac leaves can be brewed into a tea. I think I'd rather just smell them...

Lilac wood is also put to work, primarily as knife handles and musical instruments (the Greek word *syrinx*, from which *syringa* comes, means pipe or flute). Like its blooms (although some lilacs are white), the heartwood of the lilac has a slightly purple grain, and large enough trunks have been turned into bowls and walking sticks.

But, of course, it is the lilac's fragrance that sets it apart. Lilac oil is commonly used in commercial perfumes, and I have read that some people press their own lilacs to scent candles, and that lilac petals can be added directly to warm bath water for their aromatic properties. On a more nauseating note, American colonists supposedly used lilacs medicinally, often to treat intestinal worms and other parasites.

My mother loved lilacs, and she often clipped them as the weather turned warm in April. I'd come in from school to see a sprig or two sitting on our kitchen table in a canning jar, but, as far as I knew, she never used them for anything besides that simple decoration. She would, of course, be surprised to see so many lilacs so soon this spring.

It is, of course, more than just the lilacs that are blooming earlier and better, but for us, a southerly breeze has made the lilacs more obvious. I read a few weeks ago that if global warming continues unchecked, the Tidal Basin cherry blossoms we are so proud of in Washington, D.C., will be on display a full month earlier than tradition and the calendar say they are supposed to be, in another half-century or so. Our crabapples and forsythias and redbuds and dogwoods are having at it as I write this. So are the Sweet William and violets and lunaria, and my irises should be open in the next few days. It is usually midway through mushrooming season before we see much color from them, but everything these days seems to be in a hurry. Why should our trees and bushes have to wait?

My favorite reference to lilacs comes from Walt Whitman. Not long after the great poet's hero, Abraham Lincoln, was murdered in mid-April 1865, Whitman wrote "When Lilacs Last in the Dooryard Bloom'd." It is a complicated poem — three poems, really — and Whitman wrote it at a time when his own grief was symbolic of a national mourning for the martyred president.

Yet, one stanza from his poem speaks to us about the beauty of lilacs. It can surely stand alone in a spring when they are making their presence known so well. He wrote:

> *In the door-yard fronting an old farm-house,*
> *near the white-wash'd palings,*
> *Stands the lilac bush, tall-growing,*
> *with heart-shaped leaves of rich green,*

> *With many a pointed blossom, rising, delicate,*
> *with the perfume strong I love,*
> *With every leaf a miracle ... and from this bush in the door-yard,*
> *With delicate-color'd blossoms, and heart-shaped leaves of rich green,*
> *A sprig, with its flower, I break.*

I think I'll look for a canning jar now...

Make big money: Raise worms at home for fun and profit
April 16, 2012

When I think about all of the crazy things my brother and sister and I did just to make a few dollars when we were kids, I can't help but feel a little sorry for teens this summer as they try to find jobs in what is supposed to be a very tight market. Money, to say the least, was a rare commodity when we were growing up, but you have to at least give us credit for trying.

Regardless of what the kids in my classroom believe, I didn't grow up during the Great Depression. My folks, who did, were able to buy more than one pair of shoes a year for me, and my clothes weren't sewn from flour sacks. But my family was far from affluent, and I think I grew up to appreciate money, or rather the scarcity of it around our house. We were an S&H Green Stamp household; we ate out of our garden, and we drove our cars until they were exhausted, let alone out of style. I have to admit that even a trip into Terre Haute to go to Kresge's five-and-dime on Wabash Avenue or to Clinton to get a mug of root beer at the Dog-'n-Suds were, in my opinion, living large.

I eventually managed to make a few bucks when I was big enough to bale hay and feed livestock and hoe strawberries, but perhaps my first entrepreneurial venture was collecting and redeeming discarded glass soda pop bottles. I found a veritable goldmine in the ditches along the old County Line Road. I guess a lot of folks didn't think the hassle of returning bottles to their local grocery store counter for two cents a pop was worth the trouble, so, as they sped down that humpbacked blacktop past our house, they tossed their Royal Crown or Bubble-Up or Grape Nehi bottles out of their car windows. I wholeheartedly encouraged their sloth.

Despite it sounding incredibly reckless in these times, my mother allowed me to walk or ride my bike along the road to look for the bottles; then, when I managed to hitch a ride into Rosedale with my grandparents or my aunt, I'd turn them into coin at Hickman's IGA or Morgan's Variety Store, often having as much as a dime to blow on gum, orange sherbet push-ups, or Zero candy bars.

It never occurred to me to be like John Rockefeller, who, by the age of 12, had saved $10, and then earned interest on the money when he loaned it to a neighboring farmer.

No sir, I wanted the immediate rush of the sugar high that only candy cigarettes and cherry Popsicles and kissable wax lips could provide.

My brother, John, and sister, Lora, were seekers of filthy lucre, too. Sis and I sold, or attempted to sell at our roadside stand, virtually anything we could find growing on our property. We set our battered card table up under the ancient burr oak that sat near the mouth of our driveway and tried to hawk, mostly without success, walnuts, hedge apples, bittersweet and buckeyes. Nothing proved very profitable, even though both of us worked hard at appearing pathetic and malnourished for the motorists who passed by.

We also attempted to sell live bait one summer, that venture coming in conjunction with our pest control management company. Since Mom was already making us pull the bagworms off our evergreen trees once a week, we simply dropped them into old pickle jars and set up shop with zero overhead. Needless to say, containers of squirming and mildly disgusting larvae hardly put us on easy street. I don't think we sold a single worm.

Now, John was the real brains of the outfit when it came to making cash. He and my cousin, Roger, who lived across the road, spent much of their spare time carefully drawing up moneymaking plans, including the gleaning of neighboring fields for ear corn in the late fall. In those days, farmers often didn't harvest until the weather turned cold, and since the old cornpickers left a lot of corn in the fields, John and Rog were there in snotty-nosed, frozen-fingered readiness to walk the rows while they strained under the weight of their filling burlap sacks. They'd then trudge their booty into town to sell the corn at the old elevator there.

"I think we made about $2 a truckload," John told me with a smile last week as he remembered how much time and effort he had invested in the venture.

Gleaning corn was not, however, the high point of my big brother's financially formative years. He and Roger moved seamlessly into the earthworm business. Believing that my sister and I had simply failed to offer an attractive enough product, they latched onto the idea that earthworms would sell like hotcakes to the hordes of bait-needy fisherman who just happened to cruise past our house. The duo went to work digging in dozens of places around the yard, pulling worms from the soil by the dozens for immediate transfer into old, dirt-filled washer drums they'd salvaged from the dump. There wasn't a manure pile, fence row or flower bed around that they hadn't had their hands in, and in just a matter of days, the two "Earthworm Kings" believed they were about to realize fabulous profits! While the earthworms grew and prospered, the pair meandered through toy catalogs. Then, disaster struck.

The young Carnegies were crushed, not by an abnormally low bait market, but by the forces of nature. Within days, most of the worms had simply disappeared. John and Rog never imagined that worms were capable of pulling a Steve McQueen, wriggling up and over the tub walls like escaping POWs. To add insult to injury, the worms that hadn't made it to freedom, drowned when the tubs filled with water during a heavy rain shower.

Not easily deterred, the two then went into the mink-trapping business. My grandfather, who seemed to have been born in a Jack London novel, trapped muskrats all over our area, even in tiny Spring Creek, just up the road. John and Roger, lacking transportation, believed that minks undoubtedly thrived in the drainage ditch that ran across from our place. Despite the patience of Job, they snared only a few crawdads and a leech before they eventually gave up on that enterprise, too.

I could go on. My sister thought her pop bottle cap pot holders would be wildly popular, and I believed financial rewards would be mine when I got my revolutionary ant-vacuuming system worked out (ant farms were a rage then, and I would have a ready supply). My mom caught me walking out the back door with our vacuum cleaner and an extension cord before that plan could come to fruition.

The three of us kids eventually grew up, got real jobs, found our niches in life, and settled into comfortable and busy lives. None of us have made it rich, but we've never gone hungry either. We loved growing up when we did, and where we did, and we remember our nutty schemes with grins on our faces.

But I'll tell you this: If ant farms ever make a comeback, I'm going to be ready...

Getting the real lowdown on dirt
April 30, 2012

I have had my hands in the soil as of late. Two Fridays ago, I planted a viburnum bush, three chrysanthemums and a yellow poplar, not because it happened to be Earth Day, but because it was sunny and warm, and I had the whole afternoon to myself. The dirt I scraped out of and back into the shallow holes I dug near a backyard picket fence smelled good, and when dampened with a few sprinkles of water, it soon found its way into the deep wrinkles of my knuckles and under my fingernails. For the most part, I have nothing but good things to say about dirt.

There is a distinction between the two words — soil and dirt — even though we use them interchangeably.

Soil, it is said, lies under our feet, while dirt is the stuff that accumulates on unwashed hands and gets swept under rugs. For variety's sake, I will use both terms here.

The farmers have been hard at it lately, so dirt is very much on the minds of country people like us. I have seen silty clouds of it off in the distance as it is kicked up by the chisel plows and discs, and even though its scent is one I don't get as often as I used to now that so many farmers have gone to no-till planting, I caught a whiff of it in the air a time or two last week. It may sound Whitmanesque of me, but I breathed in those moments, and it kind of made me glad to be alive.

The soil around my place is mostly hard clay, although I strike a vein of good loam every so often. Rather than dig in it, I have come to know much of my dirt a chip or clod at a time.

Perhaps the hardest adjustment I had to make when I left my childhood home to live with a wife and a mortgage and an even smaller bathroom than the one we had as kids, was coming to terms with our soil. I grew up with earth so sandy and fine, and apparently rich, that transplanting a tree or hoeing a furrow for green beans or sweet corn rarely raised a sweat. I remember digging holes in our yard for my mom's rose bushes and working in my Grandpa Roy's garden, and always the soil there had a sweetness to it, a musky, pleasantness that sat in my nostrils like childhood memories now do in my head. I could have scooped a hole in that dirt with just my hands, but here at home, digging means jumping on a shovel as if it were a pogo stick. I often bank unkind words for any digging project I have to tackle.

Ironically, one of the first big jobs I had when I moved here was to replace the drains in the house. In our first winter, every elbow and trap — every inch of our drainpipes — froze as solid as stone, so I made sure when the springtime thaw came, I started at our sinks and washer and went east with new lines. Since I was keenly aware of my own poverty, I didn't hire any of the digging done, but rather grabbed an old tile spade and a shovel and a pickaxe and eagerly attacked my back yard; I think my brother-in-law, Bob, came to help me, too. I soon learned the suffering that the Chinese and the Irish immigrants who worked on the transcontinental railroad must have endured.

We had three large, old maples behind our house, and they all must have despised me, for their roots grew through every inch of the route that led me away from the house and across a fence into a pasture. To complicate matters, the house's previous owners had horses who had packed the yellow clay into something resembling a tarmac. I labored mighty and hard, and I felt that had my grandfather been alive, I would have been able to commiserate with his ditch-digging days in the WPA. Why, even moles came away with bruised snouts when they dared to dig in that area. "I dug every inch for those drains by hand," I plan to tell my grandchildren someday as we survey the property and as I describe to them my miseries and sacrifices...

I spoke of no-till farming a moment ago. It has become necessary because topsoil — that stuff we carry in the treads of our boots and the crevices of our work gloves — is only about a foot or so deep, and it tends to wash and blow away. Topsoil is where most of the growing action takes place on this planet, where plants and animals co-exist, growing and dying and replenishing. Discovery Education tells me there are more living things in a shovelful of decent soil than there are people living on the planet.

After that top layer, we find sub-soil, the stratum of dirt that contains most of the earth's minerals and water; plants point their roots downward for a reason, you know. After that comes a layer of weathered or decomposed rock, and after that, a layer of bedrock that reaches nearly to the earth's core. It was to that depth that my brother, John, and I must have been trying to reach when we were kids. Behind our house, and under a huge red oak, we had an eroded hillside that came to be known as "The Sand Pile." It was there that we dug trenches for our plastic soldiers, foxholes from which we dealt with slimy Nazis, and roads for the old metal semi-trucks we borrowed from our cousins. We eventually constructed a dugout that featured a rusting tin roof, a manhole-type door, and secret observation windows to keep a lookout for anyone daring to come our way. It is truly a wonder neither of us died in a cave-in, or struck water, whichever came first.

These days, it is called "work" when I dig in the soil, but it is now, most often, a job that I enjoy, for instead of being tied to a desk in dress shirt and shoes, I am in my jeans and boots, and I am planting something that in all probability will outlive me. This weekend, it will be an ash tree that I stumbled across in my woods last fall.

It has been said that science knows less about what goes on in the dirt under our own feet than we do about the far reaches of deep space. I guess that's true because we've always been taught to keep our heads up, rather than down. It's not a bad thing to get our hands dirty every once in a while, though.

Time to be one of the boys of
summer again
May 14, 2012

Besides writing for a living, I teach school, and I'm not ashamed to tell people that I still love my classroom. I've been a teacher for 33 years, all of them in the same school district, and virtually all of them in the same building. But I also have to tell you that if the next few weeks don't slide by pretty quickly, I may just let loose of the last thread of sanity from which I have been dangling for a while now. There are a lot of teachers out there who feel the same way.

I know, it sounds like whining; but teaching isn't nearly as easy as it looks, and it's harder now than ever before. Despite there being so many folks around who are more than happy to tell us how to do our jobs, there are precious few who would actually want to trade professions with us. Kids go just a little crazy this time of year — that gorgeous "super moon" didn't help last week — and I can't say that I blame them much: I'm a bit stir-crazy myself, kind of like the inmate who'd take work detail chopping weeds and digging ditches just to get out of his cell for a little while.

It isn't hard for me to remember my own grade school days and how antsy I was to get out of school once warm weather came calling. I loved being a kid — realized it even then — and I was always just about bursting at the seams to get away from those hard, wooden desk chairs we endured so I could get into short pants and out of shoes for a few months.

I wasn't exactly Huckleberry Finn — my mom didn't want me to have any part of rafting the river or watching gunplay in the streets — but wading creeks and skipping stones and fighting imaginary "bad guys" with sassafras sticks — complete with spittle-inducing sound effects — were activities that usually sat pretty high on my daily summer vacation agendas.

My summers were not without some education. My mom always encouraged the three of us kids to read, but books were for bedtime and rainy days and upset-stomach-on-the-couch kinds of afternoons (I usually convinced Mom that pudding would make me feel better.). We always went to Bible school and church camp, too, so I hardly turned into an unwashed heathen.

I still remember the hot summer mornings around our house that usually began in earnest after I had pushed my chair back from the kitchen table, a slop bucket-sized bowl of cereal already consumed. How happy I was to hear Mom say, "Get back to the house by noon for lunch."

I don't think I ever told my folks that it was too hot outside to play; it wouldn't have done much good anyway. Our house was shaded by a canopy of oak and beech trees, but it still got pretty warm, for we had no air conditioner, just open screened windows and old box fans. We never slept late, either; Mom wouldn't hear of it, so I was usually outside and under the shade of our trees, almost always with an army of plastic soldiers, by 8 a.m. Besides, had I stayed indoors, I'd have been given chores to do. I was certain in those days that my mother had, in a former life, been in charge of an Alabama prison work gang. So, as soon as I could, I normally blew out of the house as if it were on fire.

I do recall one summer when Mom signed me up to attend a summer school program in town, something that most would have thought I'd taken like a death sentence. But, it wasn't remedial or forced or punitive. She knew that I loved microscopes and test tubes (no, I didn't wear taped black glasses and carry a brief case), so she got me into a sort of biology camp. I loved it. About a dozen of us young intellectuals took a few trips by bus to the woods —

nothing new to me — but we also waded knee-deep into a pond to collect algae-laden water samples and hunted fossils and inspected leaves. I was never happier to step onto Glen Salmon's school bus than I was on the mornings I went into town that summer; besides, I was back home after a lunch of warm baloney sandwiches and a banana to spend the rest of the day "messing around."

When September arrived — we didn't go back to school in those days until after Labor Day — I was usually ready to head to the classroom, a new teacher, and the company of my friends, who like me, had mostly been cut off from the outside world during summer vacation. The allure of a new box of crayons and untouched notebooks, of unsharpened pencils and pristine erasers, was too much to resist, so I was usually standing near our mailbox and ready to board the bus when the time came.

This summer will be a busy one for me; I'll be back to messing around again. Oh, I don't plan to build a dam across Spring Creek or camp with my buddy, Charlie, or snag crawdads out of the ditch across the road after a good rain. I can't fish with my granddad; don't think it's advisable to climb trees or swing grapevines behind my cousins' place, either... But, I do plan to get after writing a new book, and I want to read late into the night, and put a few miles on my bike, and I want to have enough time to listen to my own thoughts. I'll become one of the boys of summer again.

Believe it or not, I'll be ready to go back to school

this August. I'll meet new students and try new lessons and get back into the groove of late-night grading and early morning liaisons with the photocopier and a slightly funky coffeemaker. I'll go back to eating my lunch out of a bag and waiting half a day at a time to run to the bathroom, and I'll tell bad jokes.

After all, I'm a teacher; that's what I do...

As of today, it's unofficially spring
March 18, 2013

Despite the calendar telling us not to rush things, I think it is all right to go ahead and say spring is here. The Ides of March has passed, Easter is coming soon, and I have already been out in my yard with a rake, getting my boots muddy. It looks like spring to me.

I have been catching myself staring out windows on these wet, gray days; it is a habit I develop as winter wears out her welcome, and my mind wanders away from my desk to visit golf courses and fishing holes and lawn mower service counters. I have moved a few short-sleeved shirts to the front of my closet, dug out a pair of sandals, even had a golf club re-gripped a few days ago, not because I can use them right away, but just so they'll be handy when they're needed.

This pre-spring is different from that of a year ago. It is wetter, for one thing. By this time last year, I noted that there was no water standing in any of the fields my wife and I journeyed past on our daily walks; in fact, violent little dust devils were sending ominous messages that perhaps a hot summer was on its way. We got the memo, sooner rather than later, and nearly ran out of sweat in the bargain.

This year, a few of the corn and bean fields near here are holding water like big brown bathtubs, the pools occasionally skimmed over with ice on the coldest nights, rippled during the day by the winds that now come more from the west and south than the north. It seems to me that most of spring's new life comes from those shallow little puddles, and from the ditches that gurgle with water that never ran in them at all until late fall last year. It will be a good year, I think, for tadpoles and crawdads and turtles. We missed them last year, and we felt cheated by their absence.

It was in a spring like this one just a few years ago that a pair of whooping cranes made an extended stop near our place. They decided they liked the fishing and frog gigging in the field ponds that were fed by an overfilled Raccoon Creek, and so, for a few weeks anyway, we got to see them from a distance as they milled about like a couple of old geezers at a shopping mall.

We have taken note that the Canada geese near our place seem to be scratching out nesting places, too, and that the trees seem to be alive with the scraggy starlings that led me to invest in a power washer a few years ago. Their contribution to the spring is less than pleasant, but if getting it here earlier means cleaning up after these freeloaders' visits, it's worth it.

It was kite-windy last week when I started to believe for real that spring was just around the corner, and despite a little rain, and a little snow, and a lot of wind, it is the memory of seeing a pair of young boys with their dad as they tossed a baseball around in their yard that has stayed with me. Within minutes of seeing them, I drove past an open produce stand, and the thought of tomatoes and sweet corn nearly made me want to skip spring altogether and go straight to summer. Nearly.

There is more to early spring than lettuce and radish seed going into the cold earth. I have seen the skin of young sassafras trees beginning to green, have already pulled a handful of early red maple buds out of my gutters where a cruel cold wind deposited them, as if warning them not to get in too big of a hurry. The moles have gotten into the act, too, tunneling near the wood line like greedy little miners looking for a big strike of grubs. The killdeer are already squawking, as well. They nag at Joanie and me as we walk by the ground they've staked out for nests later in the spring. They are excellent real estate developers, these big-mouthed little curmudgeons, but we're glad to put up with their noise.

It is an exciting time for us to walk out on our deck at night with our cats' evening meal or a few table scraps to hear the peepers down on the pond. They seem to be the true harbingers of spring, and as I've written before, it is a grand thing to know they have survived the winter snuggled in wet tree bark or under their blankets of cold leaves, only to emerge optimistic and eager to find mates and to start making house payments like the rest of us.

Spring may be springing, but I continue to feed the birds as if we had a foot of snow on the ground. This has been a good year for the jays and cardinals and woodpeckers. Just days ago, we saw three kinds of the latter — downy, red-headed and red-bellied — all dining together on sunflower seeds, cracked corn and millet with nary an argument among them. We've also watched a red squirrel come and go to the feeder all winter, his girth gradually building with his steady fix of ear corn. A young possum that I thoughtlessly named "Gary" also moved into our barn this winter, and he magically appears when he hears us filling the cat pans. These friends are addicted to our handouts, but until a spring menu of berries and bugs is posted, I have no intention of weaning them off the dole.

As reluctant as she is to get out of town, winter is history, and as the days move on, spring is dropping off notes that it is on its way. Like everyone else, I am grumbling about having to readjust my clock to New York City time just as I was beginning to see the sun breaking in the east as I drove to work. My daughter, however, has told me she has already watched a painted turtle seeking the sun on the bank of a nearby pond, and just a few days ago, she snapped a picture of an albino robin sitting in a nest near her house.

I am watching a light snow fall outside my window as I bring this story to a close. It is another gray day, and the forecast isn't calling for much more than overcast skies, and even more rainy days for a while. In my mind, though, the sky is blue, and the grass is already green.

A different kind of resurrection story; no foolin'
April 1, 2013

If you've had pets in your family long enough, it's likely that you'll see a miracle or two — a dog that couldn't possibly have lived, but did; a cat that grew to 20 pounds after being born the runt of the litter; a goldfish that had been belly-up too many times to believe it could have survived another day. But, I have to admit that when I learned of the resurrection of a dog named Bullet, I don't think I'll ever hear a pet story that will top it. Before reading on, please, disregard the fact that today is April 1, but remembering that Easter was only yesterday is appropriate.

This has not been a good year for pets around my place, and after we lost our little white-and-black barn cat — a squeaky, homely orphan named Lilly, who was unceremoniously dumped out of a moving car here years ago — my wife and I didn't think we could take on any new pets for a while. Joanie has been the tireless nursemaid to the feline sick for years, patiently caring for the sore-footed, the spayed, and the paralytic. She has spoon-fed them by the gallon, poked pills down their throats by the bottle, administered shots like a registered nurse, and emptied litter boxes by the dump truck load. In her last year, Lilly needed a lot of attention, but when it became apparent that nothing else could be done for her, we had to have her put to sleep.

Not a week after I buried Lilly — John Carradine played fewer undertakers than I have — on a hillside behind our barn, I came around the corner of our house one day to see a small black-and-white cat sniffing around our cats' food bowls.

For a second, I thought it was Lilly, for in fact, the cat was a tiny, starving stray, a Lilly clone with prettier eyes that walked right up to me as if she'd always lived with us. The look on Joanie's face when she came out of the garage door and saw me holding the cat was almost frightening; for a moment, I think she felt she was in "The Twilight Zone." Anyway, Belle is now a household fixture, whether we wanted it that way or not.

When I told that story to Katie Ferrari, a teacher friend of mine, she related a tale to me about Bullet, a small, black "Heinz 57 Varieties" kind of pup that once belonged to her mom, Velann Dorfmeyer. I knew I had to get the whole story, and Velann obliged me.

"We actually had three dogs named Bullet...," she told me. "...Bullet 1, 2, and 3. Our family home was on Highway 163, just east of Blanford, in a little area known as 'Old Jacksonville.' The highway was a very busy one, and our dogs just didn't last very long. My dad went to 'Bogleville' (another 'suburb' of Blanford) to the Davis home, and got our first Bullet. My brother was a big Roy Rogers fan, so he named the dog. Well, when the dogs met with their demise on the highway, my dad would just go back to the Davis home and get another one. Apparently, Bullet's mom was always delivering a litter," she added.

Velann can't remember whether it was Bullet 1, Bullet 2, or Bullet 3, but she assures me that one spring day she heard the screech of car tires, heard the tell-tale thud, and saw whichever Bullet lying alongside the road. Her dad (I got the impression that he was the family mortician, as well) placed Bullet in a cardboard box and buried him in the soft soil of a garden plot near their house.

"I'm sure that my brother and I cried ourselves to sleep that night, because no matter how many times it happened, we were still heartbroken," Velann says. But this is where the story got, well, downright spiritual.

"The next day was Easter Sunday (Velann's mother, who carries the rather melodic name of Carmelita Giacolleti, and who is a woman of great faith, verified the date), and we were all standing on the porch getting ready to leave for church, when we saw Bullet coming from the garden through my grandma's yard to our house. He was wagging his tail." Velann went on to add that although she and her brother were ecstatic that Bullet had sprung to life and had dug himself out of an early grave, the dog kept a healthy distance from her dad for a good while. I imagine he kept away from the highway, too.

Although we haven't had nearly as remarkable a resurrection story to tell as Bullet's, we do have another one about mistaken identity. Years ago, at a time when our local cat population was rivaling that of the Chinese mainland, we took two cats down to my in-laws, who wanted a few mousers for their barn. So, off went Bert and Ernie, a pair of gray and black brothers who had also been strays.

One day, my father-in-law, Gib, found Ernie along the road, like Bullet, the victim of a hit-and-run. He dutifully buried (I guess he was doing his best John Carradine, too) Ernie behind the barn and went to the house to tell my son, Evan, who spent most of his day with his grandparents in those pre-school years. The next day, however, as Gib stepped out of the house to feed the lonely Bert, he found Ernie waiting for his breakfast. The cat Gib had buried the day before, no doubt a transient, had just been in the wrong place at the wrong time.

Ernie's days of using extra lives were far from over, though. Later that year, after Gib and Evan had driven to a Terre Haute grain elevator with a load of corn, they found Ernie in the undercarriage of Gib's old grain truck, a bit scared by the 25-mile ride into town, but very much alive. His trip back to Parke County in the cab proved a bit more comfortable.

You know, most scientists tell us that re-animating the dead, that resurrection, is a scientific impossibility. The

Easter story, that I hope we've all heard this past weekend, and those of a "Heinz 57 Varieties" kind of dog and a scrawny black cat should convince you that it's already happened.

'Dowsers' provide hope more than science
April 15, 2013

My grandfather was a man of God. Many times I saw him, his right hand held high in the air at his Wednesday night "prayer meeting," praising the Lord before weeping at the altar on his knees. And yet, he was a "dowser," a "diviner," a "witcher" who, as a favor, would grab a forked sassafras stick and find water for some poor unfortunate whose well had gone dry.

Hydrologists, geologists, theologians, and skeptics, alike, have a hard time explaining dowsing. In an age of science and computer technology, a time in which we have solid knowledge of what lies beneath the few feet of dirt on which we trod, diviners still find steady work.

This spring, they may be out in full force, walking yards and pastures in search of a "vein" of water to tap less than a year after a drought of historic proportions hit the Midwest.

Mike Ruark, a man of science, has two degrees — one, a bachelor's in general geology, and the other, a master's in economic geology/petroleum — both from Purdue University. He says that in his line of work — that of a well driller — he's seen some things that are hard to explain, but when it comes to "water witching," he simply adds, "I have mixed feelings about even sharing what I think about it."

The art of dowsing has been around for centuries. In fact, information I found from the U.S. Department of the Interior/Geological Survey suggests that cave paintings (that are 6,000-8,000 years old) found in northern Africa are "believed to show a water dowser at work."

The tool of choice — once called a "divining rod" — was known to be used by the Scythians, Persians, and Medes. The Greeks and Romans did not mention the use of any "magic" tool," but by 1556, a detailed description of a divining rod was included in Johannes Agricola's "De Re Metallica," which outlined German methods for mining. Within just a few years, divining rods were introduced to the English, who at first used them to "locate mineral deposits," but in time used them to find water.

The same article also mentions that dowsing or witching (reputedly called such because, as another source tells me, early dowsers used witch hazel twigs in the process) eventually began to be connected to witchcraft and sorcery. Two articles condemning the practice appeared in "The American Journal of Science" in both 1821 and 1826, and at least one website that I came across likened dowsing to phony faith healings, fortune telling, and Satan's deception of man, quoting chapter and verse from the books of Leviticus and 2nd Corinthians. Yet, some dowsers themselves say that Moses dowsed for water as he "spoke to the rock," as described in the Book of Numbers.

"Even people who believe in it, can't really agree with how it is done," Ruark says. The Parke County native doesn't use a witcher, nor does he practice the art himself in his business. "I think any well driller has a very good chance of finding water in this area," Ruark added. I usually try to drill wells in a way that saves my customers the most money." As to dowsers, he adds, "I think it's almost a subconscious thing; I don't think the people who I have seen do it are faking it. I think they truly believe in it."

Finding two dowsers who witch the same way can be difficult, too. Many do use the traditional forked stick, although some swear by certain woods, with peach and willow the most popular. Some diviners use grapevines. Most want something freshly cut, although some prefer to use the same device time after time. Many dowsers have been known to use keys, wire hangers, rods, pliers, crystals, and pendulums of all kinds. Mike told me that he sees diviners using L-shaped wires, even copper tubing. The court of divining opinion is out, too, as to whether the dowser's hands need to be palm down or palm up.

The Geological Survey article was adamant that finding water may not be as difficult as it would appear. The quality and quantity of the water almost always poses a bigger problem, and from personal experience, that is undoubtedly true. I am on a municipal water line where I live, although water is in abundance in the hillside just behind my house. Because of a high sulfur content, that water isn't usable.

Diviners also tend to believe that water runs in veins — small rivers that flow or spring up. Comments I read from one dowser suggested that although he can't tell how deep the water he finds is, he can tell by the turn of his stick what direction it flows. Yet, according to the government's material, groundwater rarely ever flows in veins at all, but rather fills "pores or cracks in underground rocks."

"Well, it's kind of like arguing someone's religion or politics," Ruark says about dowsing. "But, basically, if a customer believes in it, and shows a place to me to drill, I'm going to drill a well there," he said.

I was raised in a household that hoarded water out of necessity. Despite years of sitting in the shallows of shared bath water, of rarely hosing down our flowers and grass or washing a car, and hearing the countless admonitions of my mother to always have the water "turned off tight," our well eventually filled with sand and petered out. A few hot days before a well driller came to our house packing an enormous auger and a huge concrete casement, my grandfather walked our back yard, his forked divining stick sitting lightly in his down-turned hands. As if searching for an unaccounted for land mine or a lost wedding ring, he slowly paced through the grass, clad in his undershirt and wrinkled workpants, coming closer and closer with each pass toward the driveway that was just a few feet from our back door.

He eventually came to a stop 20 feet or so from a huge red oak that sat at the base of the hill near the house, and said, as he wiped the sweat off his forehead with his ever-present hanky, "You'll get good water right here."

A few days later, the driller did just that, so much water, in fact, at 12 feet or so, that by the time he was down 20 feet, he quit digging and said that the water was pouring into the well at 25 gallons a minute, and we'd have all we'd ever need. My mom began to plant roses after that.

I don't know if what Grandpa Roy did that summer was real or sleight-of-hand or sorcery or pseudoscience. I saw the stick dip downward in his hands, yet watched it lay lifeless in my own, even when I stood on the sweet spot he'd found. For all I know, any competent well driller could have hit water there, or a hundred other places in our yard.

But for a kid who had grown up without the luxury of a sprinkler or the use of a hose, it was magic of the most divine kind.

———

A walk in the woods
April 28, 2013

I went for a walk in the woods one day last week after work. It was a warm and green afternoon, and a fresh blue breeze blew in from the west like a new spring friend. I had the intention of finding a few mushrooms — perhaps a frying pan's worth for a supper an evening or two later. My wife loves them, although I am one of those rare folks who, despite needing a minimum daily requirement of both salt and butter, thoroughly enjoy the hunting far more than the eating.

A few minutes after I had pulled into the drive to shed myself of my grown-up clothes and dress shoes, I slipped into a pair of now-not-so-blue jeans, an old ball cap, and a ratty T-shirt; I wore my most comfortable boots. Optimistically, I grabbed a few bags from our recycling box, located my favorite mushroom-hunting stick — a broom handle I've had for years — and headed down the hillside behind our barn.

It has been a discouraging mushroom season this year. I have not seen — at least of this writing, anyway — photos in the local papers of dedicated hunters standing behind the bushel baskets of morels they've found, huge grins plastered on their faces as if they'd hit the lottery.

The mushroom chatter I've heard so far has been about how far the woods seem to be lagging behind Aprils of the past, that perhaps we'll have a season that runs longer into May, that maybe this will be an off-year. I didn't get much of a positive mushroom vibe in my woods; there was simply too much bare ground about to think I'd be stumbling across a mother lode of fungus anytime soon; even my redbud trees were less than enthusiastic about showing color.

Mushroom hunting is an art, one that I'd like to think is acquired genetically, although hours of practice can't hurt. Many good mushroomers claim to be able to smell the delicacies in the air, often hunt among the decaying flesh of elm and tulip poplar trees, and are willing to crawl on hands and knees in the rain over just a few yards of earth just to get the rush of discovering a patch of the coveted sponges.

I've hunted mushrooms since before I could walk. I am told that my mom, who must have had the stamina of a longshoreman, carried me to the woods to hunt rather than do without. In fact, I come from a long line of "roomers," but discovered fairly early on that just being in the woods, whether I found a bread sack full or not, made me happy.

That was the feeling I had within minutes of walking the slopes of my woods. Fooled into thinking I'd seen a mushroom more than once by the walnut hulls and sycamore tree "buttonballs" that had been discarded by squirrels — the Oscar Madisons of my property — I decided to make mushrooms my secondary goal and just enjoy a few hours without papers to grade, problems to solve, and noises to hear.

Although my acreage is primarily one of either

descent or ascent, the woods were particularly beautiful, the late afternoon sun sifting through the newly leaved trees so that I walked in and out of shafts of warm light and cool shadows. The vivid greens of a grove of young buckeyes caught my attention, as did the bright orange of a huge splintered hedge apple tree that, like so many other trees, had dropped dead in any one of the dozen or so good winds that blew through my place over the winter. As I stood on one promontory (I live on one of the highest points in my county), I could look far into the woods, across a wetlands, to the fields beyond, accompanied by the honks of a few geese who were vying for turf on the pond below me.

I sat for a while on a blackened tree stump, staring at just a few yards of forest floor. That small bit of earth was an amazing place, really. It was a microcosm of hundreds of living things: the red ants that scrambled for cover after I had flipped a bit of sandstone on its back; the grubs surprised by the sudden sunlight; emerging ferns and hairy mosses that provided color; the now-fragile corpses of countless brown leaves being lifted by sprigs of honeysuckle and wood anemones that were trying to catch a few rays for themselves. Nearby, an outcropping of rock, spotted with gray-green lichens and musky soil, invited a look as well.

I wandered through a hillside of Mayapples, too early to have their tell-tale white blooms on display, for those come on later in the spring. In that spot, I found an

Osage-orange tree, still young, its trunk less than the thickness of my leg. It was growing out of a fallen parent, feeding itself on the dead, reaching long and hard for the soil that sat a foot or so beneath it. As I sat there, listening, thinking, mulling over nothing in particular, I spied a half-dozen young beech trees growing on a slope, a green-red chunk of stone lying nearby where it had washed down from the top of the hill. Within view, too, was a pile of slag leaf coal, undoubtedly left behind years and years ago when shallow mines dotted the hillsides. The trains, I am told, that rode the deserted and rail-less grade that now borders my land, used to stop, at least for a few years nearly a century ago, for loading from those mines. The scars of all of them are filled in and grown over now.

Before I turned for home and supper, I broke out of the woods to visit the wetlands. I spooked a notoriously crabby and long-legged Great Blue Heron and the geese that had been doing all the squawking. They all took off in a huff when I emerged from the woods, but not a green heron, who must have realized that all I was shooting was pictures. He flitted to a half-submerged log, then sat there preening and day-dreaming until I got a little too close for comfort.

I headed west and for home then, but like a late-hour shopper still searching for bargains, I inspected horsetails and cattails and dragonflies, all the while accompanied by a red-headed woodpecker that was tapping a tune and giving himself a headache a half-acre

90

away. It had been a good walk, one spent exploring grapevines and tree bark and last-year's birds' nests. I had served as cartographer of deer paths, an observer of paw paws and blue jay feathers, a meanderer and gadabout. It was time well spent.

Remembering Mom a day after Mother's Day
May 13, 2013

I don't think there has been a day in the last eight years that I haven't thought of my mom. Being all grown up with wrinkles to call my own doesn't make me miss my parents any less.

What constitutes a mom, those most remarkable of beings? What helps make our mothers protector and friend, comforter and judge, spiritual leader and homemaker? I have heard that if you want to solicit a response out of the most reticent and reserved people, ask them about their mothers, and they most certainly will have something to say. From Mary, the Holy Mother, to Mother Earth, from Mother Jones to Mother Bates, from "Mama's Family" to "Old Mother Hubbard," our culture has been influenced by the images and personalities of our mothers.

My mom was uniquely herself: She scrimped for and sacrificed for and worked for and prayed for her kids, and she loved us unconditionally. But the last thing I want to do is squeeze her into a box — into a tiny space — a "one size fits all," where one definition of motherhood tries to describe her. She had many personalities: The same woman who could wield a pretty mean yardstick when need be, liked to hold her children's hands, even when we were adults.

I recall a woman once told Mom that she didn't think it was right to embarrass me by giving me a vigorous spanking in the toy aisle of Woolworth's on Wabash Avenue; I was about seven or eight. My mother turned to the stranger and promptly told her that she should raise her children as she saw fit, but when it came to Romelle Lunsford's kids, she had better watch where she was sticking her nose. After I stopped bawling, we both laughed about the look on the old busybody's face.

We all have our own definitions of motherhood. Abraham Lincoln said of his mother, "All that I am, or hope to be, I owe to my angel mother." The writer Pearl Buck said of mothers in general, "Some are kissing mothers and some are scolding mothers, but it is love just the same, and most mothers kiss and scold together."

Famous recluse J. D. Salinger simply said, "All mothers are slightly insane," something that I would most certainly agree with. One insane mother herself, Phyllis Diller said, "I want my children to have all the things I couldn't afford. Then I want to move in with them." She also said, "We spend the first twelve months of our children's lives teaching them to walk and talk, and the next twelve years telling them to sit down and shut up."

When I think of my mom, I think of many things,

but perhaps more than most, I remember her as someone who always made sure that I was clean, that I was fed, and that I was safe. Getting dirty was more than OK with her; she wanted me to spend as much time outdoors as possible. She told me once there wasn't anything she couldn't "scrub" out of my clothes. Her fried chicken and apple pie slices (with icing) were to die for; her macaroni and cheese was pretty special, too. And, there wasn't a night that I came home late — even when I was in college — that she wasn't "still up," reading or watching a movie; she wanted to know that I was in the house before she went to bed.

I could tell a bushel basket full of stories about Mom, but one keeps coming back as I write this today. Like most parents, I suppose, my mother wanted me to be able to do things that she hadn't had the chance to do, and one at the top of her list was to play a musical instrument. My sister played the flute, and I was expected to follow in her footsteps. So, midway through my sixth-grade year, I chose the violin, which I certainly thought looked easier than hauling around a tuba. We went to the music store, picked out the model of my choice, and I promptly spent part of every other school day in the school cafeteria, of all places, under the watchful eyes and never-ending patience of our music teacher, Evelyn Vaught.

To put it mildly, I wasn't very good. I was better at applying rosin to the bow than playing a single note, and I was soon miserable, but not as miserable as Mom was. She threatened, cajoled, begged, and bribed me to practice, but as the days rolled on, I became adamant that not only could I not play the violin, I would not. Mom began taking me to Mrs. Vaught's house for private lessons, both of them believing that if I played in private that perhaps I'd relax and concentrate more. However, my crimes against music worsened, and Mom eventually waved the white flag, bought me a second-hand basketball at a garage sale, and took the violin back to the store.

I know I hurt Mom when I gave up the violin, but believe it or not, I actually loved music, even then. I just thought it sounded so much better coming from a stereo speaker than the strangled notes from that poor instrument as I punished it with my sweaty palms, tin ear, and sledgehammer touch. Other than laughing a little, Mom never mentioned the violin to me again…

A few years ago, after I had written a column in which I had mentioned dear Mrs. Vaught and Mom and my brutal attempt to master the nuances of "Ole King Cole," I told my sister that I was surprised that Mom ever had the money to spend on renting the violin and driving me to lessons in Terre Haute, and for the excessive amount of rosin that I used in preparation for my stellar performances.

"She didn't have the money," Sis told me. "She insisted that she'd clean Mrs. Vaught's house in exchange for the lessons." I have to admit, I got a little teary-eyed when I heard that.

Other than a few freshly cut irises, I can't give my mom a Mother's Day gift anymore. This story, a day late, will have to do, because I never learned to play anything but the record player.

No, there's not a day goes by that I don't miss my mom.

The 'three faces' of an Indiana spring
May 27, 2013

Indiana springs exhibit multiple personalities. They can be as soft as a warm breeze blowing through lace curtains, as cruel as the bulldozer tornadoes that slammed into an Oklahoma town last week. Just a year ago, we already suspected that a dry summer was coming with the warm air that had us in short sleeves by March. Although no one could have foreseen the scorched earth policy that Mother Nature had in store for us, I think we knew that rainclouds were going to be rare commodities for a few months.

This year has been different, yet again. We needed rain, and, of course, we got too much too soon, leaving many of us scratching our heads to wonder whether too little is better than having more than we need. If memory serves me correctly, other years have run wet out of the blocks, but have proven to be miserable finishers.

We still have plenty of time to dehydrate, and since I have already been filling watering cans this week to walk to my cone flowers and brown-eyed Susans, I fear that it may happen again this year.

Spring has been generous with us so far. I saw my first dragonflies weeks ago, and it appears to me that for the next few months, the world outside my window wants to do things in a big way. Our early cool season left my woods wet, but a bit sparse and open. I could sit at my desk-side window just a few weeks ago and look far and deep through the trees to the wetlands below us, but now, all I can see is an enveloping ocean of flickering green, every tree overloaded with new growth as if the leaves were pushing and shoving their way into the same subway car.

Because of that abundant rain, many fear we'll soon encounter mists of ravenous black mosquitoes, virulent outbreaks of West Nile, and mad rushes on department store repellent displays. But, as of yet, I haven't seen my first mosquito, even in the early evening as I mow near the wood line where I donate a few pints of blood each summer.

The creepy red-and-black boxelder bugs are another thing altogether. They are having a heyday at my place — and I suspect at yours, as well. They are everywhere, ushering themselves uninvited into the house at the opening of every door and window. From what I hear, they are particularly bothersome in years following unusually dry summers, and they won't go away until the weather turns cold again. Their mere presence is bad enough, particularly when I feel one trundling its way through my hair or under my shirt collar; they seem to have a special affinity for landing in my face, too. More repulsive are their amorous endeavors as they cling to the siding of my house — it's enough to make Caligula blush.

The butterflies are now here, too. Already, I have seen big swallowtails flitting from one iris to another, so I filled a birdbath yesterday, just to give them a drink when they tire of the sweaty, desperate work of searching for pollens and nectars. Every flowering bush and tree I have has exploded; my grass is as green as any football field's artificial turf, and the ditches grow wild and high with ivies and weeds that normally need no mowing for weeks to come, particularly last year when their scruffiness just grew more depressing as the months passed.

The whirligigs are doing their thing, as well. Lately, I am raking them up by the bushels, blowing them from our gutters, and brushing them from our walks. They are a pleasant nuisance, helicoptering their way across my lawn in the breeze, rattling like dry corn as they skitter across the concrete. They scritch and dance into the most surprising places, and after a little rain, they sprout shoots like soy beans, creating, unless I pull them up, a billion tiny silver maples.

Unless it is the cottonwoods, nothing, it seems to me, has enjoyed the weather this spring as much as the black locust trees. Just a few days before we picked up what was left of the terrible winds that raked Oklahoma, the trees were bursting with fresh white fragrant blooms, so many that from afar, the ridgeline that runs up the valley to our north looked as if a freak snowfall had blanketed us. The blooms looked a little less lively after the winds, but I can still stand near my front door and pick up the scent from a grove of locusts a few hundred yards away. The blooms' scent, mingled with that of my lilacs and irises, has communed enough to make an open window even more inviting than usual.

I have had an uneven relationship with locust trees. Both of the most common kinds here in Indiana — black and honey — were abundant where I grew up. More than once I have stepped on the thorns of the latter — punctured several tractor tires with them, too. When we first moved here years ago, we had two huge old locusts looming over our house, but we eventually had to have the trees cut down, for both were splitting at their seams. For years, I fought the sprouts from their remaining roots, like Leonidas at Thermopylae, only I was manned with a scythe. Walking my yard every few days, I'd whack the young trees as they popped up through the grass. And then one summer, they just quit showing up.

Black locusts are considered an "invasive species," although they may have been native to the far-southern ends of the state. They can wreak havoc on forests, crowding out more desirable trees with their impressive sun-robbing crowns. But they are prized by loggers, and there doesn't seem to be any organized effort under way to wipe them out. In fact, they were originally planted in Indiana because of their abundant lumber, used years ago for fence posts and wagon wheels. They are fast-growing trees, often reaching 80 to 100 feet in height. Locusts are pollinated by bees and hummingbirds, and the bobwhites, mourning doves, wild turkeys, white-tailed deer, and squirrels swear by salads made from the seeds, twigs, and leaves.

For most of the year, our locust trees are kind of a nuisance. They are thorny and trashy trees, dropping bits of themselves at the hint of a breeze. Their seeds are hidden in long ugly brown pods that look like old arthritic fingers, and they split and fall at the most inopportune times. But for this few weeks in the spring when they are in bloom, locusts are one of my favorite trees. I have the open windows to prove it.

Mike Lunsford

~Summer~

"Summer is a promissory note signed in June, its long days spent and gone before you know it, and due to be repaid next January."

Hal Borland

It's true: 'There's no place like home'
June 13, 2011

My wife and I hadn't been into town for a good while when we drove in from our place to visit her doctor and my favorite hardware store last week. After her appointment and my aisle-wandering were done, we topped off our gas tank, ate a nice lunch, and headed for home. Along the way, we got a chance to see firsthand the damage just a few minutes of wind can do.

As we drove through the north end of town, we gawked at the aftermath of the storm that hit our area several weeks ago. Open-mouthed, we took in blocks of splintered trees and tarped roofs, fractured gutters and busted windows, and realized just how lucky we had been in losing only our pretty little Bradford pear tree and the top of one of our Georgia red pines to the storm. I was able to clean up our messes in a few hours of bending and sweating, and sawing and dragging, but much of what we saw that day in town won't be cleaned up for months to come.

The devastating images we've seen out of Tuscaloosa and Joplin on the evening news made nervous wrecks out of a lot of folks before the thunderstorm ever came our way in the reds and yellows of a radar screen. I've caught myself peering out windows more often this spring, glancing skyward and standing in the kitchen to wait for the weather report to show up on the television.

I've replaced the batteries in our weather alert radio, too, just in case we lose power. I was brought up having a healthy respect for storms; it didn't take much thunder or wind to convince my mom that we all should head to the basement, and in my memory's eye, I can still see the rain battering against the long, narrow windows that lined the damp, dark cellar of my childhood house as we huddled together near its creaky stairway. I remember the crack of the lightning that felled a huge red oak that stood near my grandparents' drive, and can still feel the house shudder under the weight of it crashing to the ground.

Scientists tell us that storms are going to be more frequent in the years to come, more violent, too. I want to believe they are wrong, but suspect they aren't. I want to think that since there are more people now than ever before — housing developments seem to pop out of the ground like mushrooms to hold all that humanity — storms no one noticed decades ago now pack more costly wallops. The odds that people and bad weather can avoid one another have now grown against us. I hope against hope that one reason we hear about more storms is because we have the technology to see them and track them and report them better. But looking at the Hiroshima-like settings that used to be vibrant parts of towns in Alabama and Missouri, I can't help but believe that we are having more storms, and that they are growing worse. I fear that the next time, we could lose more than just our electrical current and a few limbs.

We moved to our home nearly 30 years ago. Joanie was just a few days shy of having the baby who would turn out to be our daughter, Ellen, and we needed more room. A friendly couple named Freeman and Wilma Chaney offered to sell us their place on contract, since just about everyone around knew we wanted a house, but couldn't afford the 16-percent interest rates the banks were "offering" in those days. I knew absolutely nothing about buying a house, and after waltzing through the place in just a few minutes, not even stopping to look at the furnace or the plumbing or the condition of the roof, we agreed to buy it. I used my father-in-law's grain truck to help move the Chaneys out and us in, and we haven't budged since.

Over the years, we have done the usual remodeling that accompanies stability and a few raises in pay. Nearly 10 years ago, we added a family room and a new bathroom and a deck. The house has been re-roofed twice, has been re-carpeted, and we have a relatively new kitchen. I propped our old barn up and have given it numerous coats of paint; we built a storage barn, and a cabin, and I have hacked and sawed away brush for years to carve out an expansive rolling yard that runs head-long into the 15 acres of woods we now share with frogs and raccoons and deer.

Our home isn't perfect; it awaits more replacement windows, and we hope to remodel two bedrooms soon. A number of the pine trees that I planted within just a year or two of moving here have died, as have those of my neighbors, and I now have to cut them down with the memories of walking five-gallon buckets of water out to them still in my head.

We love the woods here; we love our hummingbirds and our trees and our clean air and our ever-present breeze. We don't live in a palace, but we don't owe much on it, either. It has become our home, our refuge, a place that aggravates us at its worst, but comforts us at its best. It is the place where we have chosen to stay.

Our homes are more than shingles and concrete blocks and 2-by-4s; they are more than a mortgage at the bank and a place in which we store furniture and hang clothes. We need to appreciate what we have more often, to be thankful for it, and to help others who have lost what we often take for granted.

After she was swept away in a Kansas tornado, Dorothy Gale finally discovered that "there's no place like home." After awakening from her dreams of Oz, she says, "...if I ever go looking for my heart's desire again, I won't look any further than my own back yard. Because if it isn't there, I never really lost it to begin with!"

And to think, it took a storm to make her realize that...

———

The tale of the lonesome pines
June 27, 2011

As I sloshed a can of water over a pot of red petunias a Sunday morning ago, I saw a pine sawyer beetle make its way slowly up the vinyl siding near my front door. I swatted it to the concrete, and smashed it with my shoe ... with impunity, I might add.

I don't have a problem with most insects at all. Sure, I've just about had it with the wasps that keep building their nests over and over in my hose reel box and menace us as we water our tomatoes, and I have wood bees snooping along the eaves of my cabin, which I now inspect almost daily. We faced an ant invasion in our kitchen this spring, too — a little spraying and a lot of vacuuming took care of it — and we occasionally find in the garage those huge wolf spiders that send shivers up our spines. But, for most part, we live with the bugs around our place, taking the good with the bad. We enjoy our dragonflies and butterflies and the occasional praying mantis, and I mow slowly when the clover is in bloom just so our honey bees are given a chance to get out of the way. I hear that the walking sticks we always have near our porches are pretty good at eating bad bugs, so we leave them alone, too. Like everyone else, we tolerate the gnats and the black flies and the mosquitoes.

Sawyer beetles — also called long-horned beetles — are a whole different story. Not only are they repulsive-looking little buggers, they are the main reason I am cutting down most of the Georgia red pines on my property, trees that I planted 25 years ago to serve as windbreaks and natural privacy fences. The beetles not only have the rotten habit of feeding on the young pine shoots, which causes enough damage, but they also release hitch-hiking nematodes — tiny worms — from their breathing pores that go on to chew on the already wounded tree until its needles turn brown, its bark peels off like sunburned skin, and the tree dies a slow, creeping death.

When we first moved here, the only trees that had ever really been planted on the property were a few fast-growing locusts and soft maples. Within a year or two, we had to cut down a massive, dying sycamore in our front yard, and one of the locusts blew over in a storm. I made up my mind that I was going to plant more trees as I expanded and groomed my yard, and I did just that, sticking pin oaks and tulip poplars that have grown and prospered and shaded us just about everywhere we can walk.

Since we own a large, long front lawn, and the wind blasts across it from the fields to our west, I decided to plant a windrow of pines to cut the current down a bit. I ordered trees from the state Department of Natural Resources, and when debating as to whether I should order red or white pines, was told by a naturalist there that the white pines were more common but the red pines were hardy and would be more distinctive. I took his word for it and planted 24 of them along the roadside; the sawyer beetles must have paid him under the table ...

The trees grew like weeds. For a few years — since I was living on a young teacher's salary and couldn't shell out the money for the quarter-mile length of garden hose I needed — I walked five-gallon buckets of water to the trees. I pulled the weeds around their trunks by hand to protect them, and kept them fed with fertilizer. Within a few years, I was mowing around their broadening bases, amazed that they were getting so large and full and green.

Then the assaults began. The trees weren't helped when a county road crew sliced into their roots as they "bermed" the ditches along my place with a road grader. A year or two later, a speeding driver managed to run off the pavement and whack into three of them. Over the years, wind blew the tops out of a few more, and it didn't take long before the deer began to nibble on and rut against the rest. I have accidentally smacked into them with mowers and weed trimmers, and they have been pelted with sand and salt and rocks via the snowplows, but somehow, the pines thrived. That is, until pine wilt took over, caused by the pine sawyer beetles.

I hoped that somehow the trees would make it. I trimmed them religiously, first at their bases, then at eye level, and eventually from a ladder. I sprayed and fertilized and worried, but, one by one, the trees became skeletal and brown, and in even the slightest breezes the limbs dropped messily into the yard. Long, dry Indiana summers are particularly hard on red pines, so last year's drought had to have been a contributing factor to my trees' rotten health.

A few Saturdays back, Zach Sampson and Torre Lynn, two former students of mine who don't think going to work is enough work to work at, dropped by. I had told them that I wanted to take out the dead pines, and they reminded me that they were up for the job since they both dearly love their chainsaws, making a few dollars and working together. I told them that six of the trees still looked pretty good, nine were on the critical list, but would be given a last chance, and nine had to be cut and hauled off. Within five hours, the trees were felled, cut into pieces, hauled off and burned (infested wood should be torched). They even raked up the lawn before they left. As I wrote out a check, I told them that the pines remaining on life-support would probably have to go by the end of the summer, and that I'd be calling on them again.

In the days since the trees were cut, I have missed them. That may sound silly, but I can't help but mow the yard and notice the sun beating down where there was once shade or hearing the road noise that was once muffled. I know the pines I have left will have to go, and I think that once I get their stumps out of the way, I'll probably plant crabapples or redbuds or dogwoods — something that won't get too big and will add color to my yard. Ironically, I have planted a number of white pines around my place, and they are tall and healthy and green. White pines rarely contract pine wilt.

Much has changed since I first planted my red pine

trees. I know I don't have the desire to haul water two buckets at a time to what will be growing out there next, and I know it was easier on my creaky back to have those two young guys doing the cutting and lifting, raking and sweating on that humid Saturday afternoon, too.

But if I happen to see another pine sawyer beetle anywhere on my property, he's all mine ...

Listening to the sounds of silence
July 11, 2013

I have visited this topic — how it is often only through inconvenience that we come to appreciate the comforts we have in life — before.

I guess I needed to be reminded of that again last week when a late-night thunderstorm came plowing through our area, zapping phones and computers and garage door openers and, eventually, our own electrical power.

In an instant, my wife and I lay in our bed in the dark, in silence, listening...

I had retired to read around 11:30, the late local news over, an impromptu bowl of cereal still sloshing in my stomach. Tired and a bit back-sore after a day of mowing and weed-whacking in the Turkish steambath-kind of heat that comes to stay with us in July, I peeked through our west-facing windows as I hobbled off to turn a few pages of a book that needed to interest me that night or find itself in a garage sale box.

I commented to Joanie that we either had a whopper of a thunderstorm headed our way or a fireworks show in the northern corner of the county was running late, because the sky was restless with flashes of light.

Because storms had become as regular for us as a daily vitamin, regardless of what the weatherman was predicting, we expected to find an inch or so of rain in the gauge on my cabin porch rail the next morning; we weren't disappointed.

I wearily turned only a few pages of the book before I clicked off my light and went to sleep.

My wife, as she often does, had read in her living room recliner until her chin was on her chest, and was stumbling into the bedroom an hour behind me as the lightning and wind and rain were coming on in earnest. I was awake by then, and she told me that our deck table umbrella had come unmoored and had blown against our back door. I launched myself out of bed to retrieve it, knowing it could be in the jet stream over Bridgeton by morning.

I don't sleep well when wind and rain are driving by my place, but I usually can't sleep at all when lightning and thunder are along for the ride. I tried to read with my booklight for a while as I heard the rain smacking down on our roof and pelting our storm windows, and I kept hopping out of bed to unplug the victims of earlier lightning strikes, our computer, for example. I was headed for our phone just as a brilliant blue-white bolt struck in the field across from the house, setting off our smoke detectors and dimming our lights in a scene reminiscent of a prison-break movie.

Back in bed for what I hoped would be the last time that night, I believed that I'd eventually be too tired to stay awake for long, that the worst of the storm had already passed, and that the hum of our bedroom fan would lull me away from the worries of ripped shingles and overflowing gutters and a now-messy yard.

It didn't work out that way; the storm returned for another assault, and then another, and another. And then, in the eerie, flashing light of countless strikes, our power died. I heard the last gasp of our air conditioner, the fan went dead, and the blinking blue light of our computer modem flickered and passed away in the living room. Suddenly, a house that had been alive with the purrs of a refrigerator and a dish washer and a hot water heater was as quiet as a tomb, completely dark, except for the craggy streaks of nature's pyrotechnics.

I read a "Newsweek" magazine article a month or so ago that suggests that Americans are now hearing so much, seeing so much, overloading their circuitries with so much information and sound nearly every minute of their day, that they can't make good decisions anymore.

It was far from a clinical study that night, but it didn't take a minute for that thought to drift through my mind. I had become so used to hearing something — the drone of a fan; the canned laughter of a television; the clack of keyboard keys a room away — before I drifted off to sleep each night that total silence in the house was unsettling. I couldn't sleep...

The storm spent itself and was gone within a half-hour more, but the house grew so quiet, so hushed that it took me back to grade school sleepovers with friends and how I always struggled to sleep in strange places. My wife, who, I'm certain, can fall asleep in a chainsaw repair shop, was already snoozing, the rhythm of her breathing now louder than normal. I grabbed my pillow and a blanket from under the bed and headed for the couch.

As I settled on the sofa, I heard little but the ringing in my ears; I rolled and tossed, and eventually moved to the floor of our family room, slightly warm and agitated. I asked myself how I could spend so much time in my cabin, never missing the television or the stereo, most often just listening to the thoughts in my head or the birds through the screened windows, and being comforted by just those few sounds, yet this near-total silence exasperated me. The hours dragged by endlessly.

By 5 a.m., I had done a lot of thinking, but virtually no sleeping. The whole thing kind of reminded me of a scene from an old W.C. Fields' film, "It's a Gift," where the hapless protagonist, Harold Bissonette, tries to grab a few minutes rest on a back-porch swing, but his harpy wife, an ice-pick wielding Baby Leroy, an overbearing insurance salesman searching for Carl LaFong, and a rolling coconut all conspire to see it doesn't happen. I had no squeaking clotheslines or obnoxious neighbors keeping me awake, like Bissonette, but the usual cracks and creaks of a cooling, settling house had become klaxons to me.

By 6 a.m., the sun began to make early ventures through the clouds, just enough, I might add, to shine through the blinds into my face.

It was irritating, but by no means did the light keep me awake as much as the robins in the maples just a few feet and a wall away. Apparently happy to be out of their nests and up for a day of grooming my lawn for worms, they were cheerfully and loudly discussing the day's business.

By that time, our old housecat, Arthur, was also into the act. Hungry from a night spent in the garage in his own bed, he was clawing at our door, wailing in hopes of his usual monotonous breakfast. With his pitiful cries, I gave up any illusion of sleep, so I slipped on a pair of jeans and headed out the door to the newspaper box.

The power was restored by 8:30. I knew the crew of utility linesman spent a much more restless night in their work than I did in my attempt to slumber, but I can't imagine that they felt any worse for wear.

All at once, our house was filled with the beeps and murmurs and whistles of freezers and ceiling fans and microwaves coming to life. Within minutes, I heard ice cubes automatically plopping into a plastic tray.

At some point in my sleepless vigil, I contemplated how just a few generations ago people went to bed and slept and awoke to silence in their homes, and how the conveniences I had in a "modern" life, when taken from me for just a few hours, had made me dependent on comforting sounds, like a baby who hears its mother's heartbeat in the womb.

I thought I loved silence, and I know I have been critical of so many as they've passed me with wires plugged into their heads, their music so loud I could hear it myself. But I seek silence of my own choosing.

Late that afternoon, bleary-eyed and thick-headed, I lay down on our bed for a quick nap. Just to be sure, I flicked on the fan; I had to hear something.

Overheated in Hobart and other vacation tales
July 25, 2011

My family climbed into our van and headed to Michigan a few weeks ago, just as we do every other year or so, to stay on the great lake there, for we have come to love its cool breezes and blue water and lighthouses.

It was a fever blister of a morning as we packed too much gear into our wagon and drove north, our onboard thermometer already showing off a nasty 95 degrees before noon, but we wiped the sweat off our foreheads and settled into a not-so-unpleasant four-hour drive to the land of beach sand and low humidity.

We had no problems whatsoever as we peeled off the miles through the flat, endless fields of corn and wind turbines in Benton and Newton counties, driving through Kentland and Schneider and Lake Station on the way to I-94 and the last leg of our journey. We stopped for gas and a bite to eat, stretched our legs, and soon dove into the five-lane madness of semi-tractor trailers and boat-toting pick-ups just as the day's heat peaked at 97, content in our refrigerated front-wheel drive cubicle. Then, we smelled trouble — literally.

It came in the way of our front brakes locking up. The constant stopping and starting on the crammed interstate apparently put the finishing touches on a brake system that had ironically been inspected and declared "good to go" at a local garage just a few days earlier. We limped to a stop, managing to drag ourselves off the main road to an off-ramp, our right front wheel sizzling and smoking.

We keep a roadside service plan for such emergencies, so I took cell phone in hand and called its number. Due to "heavier than usual" business, I was told by machine before I ever spoke to a human being, it would be 90 minutes to five hours before anyone could come to assist us. After being cut off a time or two, I reached a young lady who seemed to be much more concerned about the color of our van than actually getting someone out to help us drive it, so instead of sitting along the road like an ant under an hourglass, I decided to creep our crippled wheels into the next town that happened to be along Indiana 6. It was Hobart.

I took the first left turn off the down ramp into town and immediately saw a huge brown sign that miraculously read "Brake and Muffler Repair," so we crawled into the baking parking lot that sat beneath it. Within minutes, the problem was assessed, an estimate was delivered, and despite it being past 4 in the afternoon and all of the shop's bays filled with other disabled cars, an already soaked and tired technician named William had our van up on a jack, its calipers and brake pads and metal lines dropping to the pavement at chop-shop speed.

What one does on the outskirts of Hobart with no transportation proved no conundrum: We sat and waited. But as unpleasant as that sounds, the five of us — my son's fiancé, Lucy, went along — actually had a good time. We found a little shade under an awning, catching an occasional whiff of breeze, and we talked, and took part in the fine art of observation. I struck up a conversation with a lady who works as a cook at the local high school; she was concerned that her car's transmission was kaput, but after numerous test drives, nothing could be found wrong with it. She left us with wishes that our repairs wouldn't cost much and hopes for a better day.

By the time William was wiping the grease off his hands, co-manager Pete had done a test drive, and fellow co-manager Jim had us swiping plastic at the cash register; we were back on the road by 5:30, my credit card doing the smoking by then. But I have a lifetime warranty on that new brake system, by the way, and we were driving again.

Life was good.

Within two hours, we stood on a breezy Lake Michigan beach, and in contrast to that sweltering asphalt in Hobart, I felt as though we were a world away. On that first evening, we were drawn to the water like moths to a back porch light, and we all waded and walked and gazed and sighed with our sandals in our hands until hunger drove us up the hill to supper and a bath and a bed (although they proved too small for this reasonably tall writer and his even taller son).

Early the next day, we returned to the beach, and I began a too-short string of days sitting in a chair, book in hand, feet buried in the sand; it was as ambitious as I wanted to get. In the time I spent in that place, and in the solitude that the sounds of the crashing waves helped me find in my own head, I tried to count the shades of blue reflected in the lake. I became a watcher of wind-blown marram grass, an observer of shorebirds, and a collector of round, smooth stones. I often gazed upward to see small glints of silver flying thousands of feet above us, but doubted that anyone on those jets was going anywhere I would rather be at the moment. I soon became interested in watching a sailboat that ambled along the horizon, its snow-white sail cutting a path across a bank of deep blue, and I heard Frank Sinatra crooning "Summer Wind," despite there not being a radio in sight.

There was much to do besides read and work crosswords and tell my wife how pleased I was we were back at the lake. I watched a woman pull a Keystone Kops routine as she chased down a runaway beach umbrella and spied a Tony Siragusa look-alike drifting in the surf, the waves pounding his considerable bulk like a forlorn buoy. I observed people who, like my clan the day before, came out to the water for the first time, standing and staring out at the horizon. Like us, I suppose, that endless expanse of water drove them to dreams and deep thoughts and lower blood pressures.

The shorebirds kept us entertained. I wondered more than once how the big white and brown gulls could hover in one place without moving a wing as the wind blew straight off the lake so hard it threatened to tear my book's pages. A flock of them — hundreds, I believe — landed en masse some 75 yards from us, bobbing in the waves like white apples in a blue-green barrel. They eventually took off together and headed north before testing the waters again.

I noticed that as the days wore into evenings, and the sun played tricks with its angles, that the water turned to bronze. I would occasionally take a short walk to stretch out the kinks in my legs and soon learned that not all on the lake was timeless and pleasant. The flotsam brought onto shore held an odd mixture of the natural and the man-made. Among the tiny brown shells and water-worn rocks was the detritus of the careless and uncaring. Cigarette butts and wads of gum, a rubber band and a length of balloon ribbon, the useless tubes of exploded fireworks and a long-drained beer can, all brought me back, for a few minutes anyway, to the messes people often make of such a place.

As we drove home a few days later, groggy from sleeping in strange rooms, too red from too much time in the sun, and tired from our long and full days, I could still see that stretch of beach and hear the rhythm of those endless waves, even as I maneuvered the highway lunacy that carried me away from it.

I daydreamed about that blue water for a long time, but I was just as thankful that we found a steam bath of a brake shop in Hobart, too.

Reading is reading, but a bookstore is a joy
August 8, 2011

I wandered into the local mall bookstore the other day. My wife and I had come to town with a list of chores to do and things to buy, but whenever we venture anywhere near a place with book shelves and sales tables and racks of paperbacks, we're attracted to the scent of ink and the sight of book covers like bees to clover .

The store in question, a Waldenbooks/Borders, is closing; it has been there since there was a mall, and the people I have come to know who work there are sad, not just because they're out of a job, but because a place they have come to love will soon be gone.

Since I didn't ask to use their names in this story, I won't, but I do remember an impromptu conversation with one of the managers that hot afternoon, and she was clearly upset. She said one of the very best things about her job — she has been there for over 20 years — was seeing kids in the store with their parents, or even on their own, wandering around, mouths agape, picking and choosing and enthusiastically looking at books. She said she will miss that most of all.

I know, I know; we need to get with the times. The latest rage of e-readers has rendered real books made with paper passé. They are, we are reminded over and over again, old-fashioned, environmentally disastrous, bulky, space-wasting and expensive.

We need to get on board, charge our batteries, download a good book and quit whining, because we can't swim against the tide that technology has sent to our beaches. Besides, books aren't going to go away, we are told; just the way we access what we read is changing.

I am comforted by that, but I wonder about the value of the bookstore — the actual place — where books, in any form can be found.

Why the store is closing is pretty obvious. The entire chain, of which this bookshop is just one of 399, is closing all of its doors. Bemoaned by reading purists 40 years ago that it was the cause of so many small, independent bookstores blowing away in a wind of change, the company has not kept up with the times and has been put out of business. My fear now is that there will be fewer and fewer places to go to buy books, other than through the web, of course. I have no argument against that practice either, for I have gone that route too, finding books that hide in warehouses from coast to coast and having them shipped to my door.

In all probability, I will buy an e-reader someday, a Nook or Kindle or whatever new item may soon come down the pike, and I'll do it without losing sleep.

I have to admit that it is enticing, perhaps even smarter, for me to invest less than five hardback books' worth of reading capital into a hand-held e-reader. I'll have selection and sales at my fingertips, and I won't have to walk into a bookstore and hope someone helps me, or glance over countless books, hoping I'll find one that piques my interest. I won't need to ramble through a field of sale books anymore, or strike up a conversation with someone doing the same thing. I'll miss it all.

I like books. I think about them often, buy them often, enjoy seeing them on my shelves. I am reading a particularly good book right now as the result of my last trip to the store. Just a few days ago, as I made my way from my car to the front door of my doctor's office, book in hand — for one never knows how long he'll have to wait there — I dropped it. I'm happy that in that instance I didn't own an e-reader, or I'd have been sweeping my book into a trash bag.

We should not be singing dirges for reading just yet; statistics show that people who own e-readers actually buy more books than those who don't. People are buying millions of them online, probably the main reason the mall store and its cousins nationwide died. No, finding a book, even pretty obscure titles, is easier than ever before. I do wish more kids were reading though.

Reading is alive and kicking; it's the bookstore itself that is in trouble. With fewer outlets, big and small, readers have fewer choices, and because of that, publishers are narrowing the field, printing more copies of fewer titles. James Carroll wrote in a recent column for the Boston Globe: "An industry that had thrived on a wild diversity of taste and a near-infinite supply of manuscripts, mostly published in relatively small print runs, became ever more uniform, and ever more closed to all but big-name authors and potential best-sellers."

Michael Dirda saw the writing on the bookselling wall five years ago when he published "Bound to Please." (Yes, it is available for download.) In it, he said, "To my mind, the real literacy crisis has less to do with the number of people reading than with the narrowing range of literary and intellectual works that Americans actually read. More and more have been straight-jacketed and brainwashed by the books of the moment, the passing moment."

Although it seems as though I never run out of books to add to my "want list," I am worried that there will be fewer places to buy them. Locally, we are still fortunate to have as many bookstores as we do; several of them even sell my books. I worry a bit, though, that over the next few years, I am going to have fewer bookstores to wander and explore. I wonder, as well, that if e-readers become the medium of choice for reading, what will happen to children if they or their parents can't afford them. I am presuming that the price of such things will continue to drop, but I also think it would be difficult to find sale tables filled with used technology for a dollar or two. For that reason alone, I hope that parents help their children become better acquainted with a local library.

The facts about reading and books and bookstores are mixed. A recent article at LiveScience.com touts a study by the University of Nevada that found that children who are raised in average homes with average incomes, but who have at least 500 books in the house, on average, attained at least three more years of education than those with no books. Another study found that people who read traditionally made books read them twice as fast as those who read them electronically.

But, the cold, hard fact remains: We are killing off traditional bookstores, and those of us who love them, including those folks I know who will be working for only a month or so at one, had better just read it and weep.

———

Mike Lunsford

The annoyance of life's little conveniences
August 22, 2011

I am aware that much of the language I use is outdated, stodgy, old-fashioned; I apologize.

So, when I tell you that I pulled my truck into a "gas station" last week to fill up, please understand that I mean a "convenience store" or "express mart." A guy has to work pretty hard these days to find a real gas station, one where the owner has grease under his fingernails and a name tag sewn onto his shirt.

Anyway, I proceeded to do what I most often do at the gas pump; I jabbed my credit card into a slot, pushed all of the requisite buttons — including those that constituted my zip code — got the official OK, then proceeded to watch in irritation as big numbers rolled up in the "total sale" window.

I use a credit card at the gas pump for convenience. Because I do, I don't have to stand in a line at the cash register, don't have to sign anything, and I get a rebate on my purchases.

But, as in many cases these days, I've discovered that what is "convenient" has its inconveniences too. I am not exaggerating when I say that most of the time when I fuel up and "pay at the pump," I end up walking into the store to get the receipt anyway. Most often, I am told, "That pump hasn't been giving receipts," or "I guess we need to get paper in it," or "We don't know what's wrong with that thing."

The short walk to the counter isn't going to kill me; I'm not one of those people who cruises a parking lot for 15 minutes to find a parking spot a few feet closer to the door. I know I could drive off without a receipt, but, as a creature of habit, I want one.

After all, who hasn't had to make a call to the credit card company at one time or another over some kind of a miscalculation or billing error?

Everywhere we go these days, we are told that things are being done for our convenience. Drive-up here, press "1" or "2" there; it's all being done so our lives will be easier and faster and more efficient. And if you believe that, I have some prime real estate to sell you. What once used to be done by living, breathing people is now controlled by automation, by that almighty god, Technology.

A few years ago, I wrote about the Luddites, a group of 19th century textile workers who came to oppose technology — sometimes violently — not because they thought it was sinful or the work of the Devil, but rather because they believed mass production and mindlessly repetitive factory work were detrimental to economies and product quality and, of course, to a dispirited and enslaved workforce.

I am, most decidedly, not a Luddite. I understand that many of the products I buy and use are reasonably priced and abundant because they are not made by highly skilled and expensive technicians. But is it too much to ask to actually speak to a human being when I want to discuss a bill? Is it unreasonable to get someone to replace a roll of paper at a gas pump or to walk into a store from which I purchased a product and not be told that their service center is located in Sri Lanka?

I suppose that there's a price to pay for all of us whose births pre-date the majority of the technologies we live with and depend upon. My children and my students, who often are amazed at my limited knowledge of the latest things hand-held or plugged in, will sooner or later realize that they, too, are slipping behind the electronic curve.

There's no doubt that I enjoy the crystal clear television reception I receive via satellite dish, that is, unless it rains. Give me a brief cloudburst or a bit of lightning, and I'm watching a quiet blue screen. A few years ago, we were mandated to switch from an analog to a digital signal, a taller order for those folks who live in rural, isolated areas. A relative of mine lost free television for good. It was either put in a satellite dish or employ Gustave Eiffel to design a tower tall enough to pull in the local channels.

Just a few days ago, I took my cell phone into a store to ask about a new battery. The clerk (a polite young guy) told me that my model — a whopping four years old — was "outdated," and they "didn't even sell that battery anymore." He told me I was looking at an upgrade, or perhaps I could find a battery online. Four years old is old?

Perhaps the best illustration of what I mean came

to me a couple of weeks back. My mother-in-law needed a new window air conditioner, so my wife and I volunteered to pick one up and install it for her. Appropriately, it was hotter that day in local store parking lots than the actual surface temperature of the sun, and after stops at three or four stores that had no window units left, Joanie decided to use her cell phone to save time and fuel and frustration.

After several fruitless calls, we took off for the south end of town anyway. While I drove, her call to one local store got her re-routed to a "convenient calling center" in Florida. By the time she received word that the store in question did, indeed, have a few of those rare units in stock, I had driven four miles through traffic, parked the car, walked into the store, and had asked two sales clerks about amperages and BTUs and prices.

From automated checkout aisles at grocery stores (surely designed by Rube Goldberg) to the ATM machines that eat cards to the fast-food drive-thru lanes with speakers manned by Charlie Brown's mush-mouthed teacher, give me convenience. After all, I have places to go and things to do with all the time I'm saving, that is, unless I'm put on hold ...

The value of hard work goes beyond a paycheck
September 5, 2011

Years ago, I used to drive into Rosedale to get my workday started with a big cup of black coffee. Every morning, Monday through Friday, until the town grocery store's business dried up and blew away, you could have found me slipping through a back door — left unlocked for the early birds — of the old Red and White, 15 minutes before it opened for official business. I'd quickly pour a travel mug of hot determination, leave my quarters on the counter, and speed off to face the classrooms and quizzes and organized chaos of a school day. I miss it.

I make my coffee at school now, sharing it with a few of my teaching buddies, and I do it well before most of my co-workers get to work, the parking lot quiet and growing darker as these weeks pass into fall. I like to be there early in the morning, like to get after my jobs right away and in solitude. It's just the way I am.

But I do miss running into town for my coffee, perhaps stopping for a moment's conversation with Wendell Jenkins, who often beat me there to get his day under way with a plate of biscuits and gravy. I also noticed that nearly every morning a pair of men, sometimes in heavy winter overalls, shuffled into the bakery to eat breakfast and gab and smoke before their workday started. I knew they'd be working a lot harder than I would that day — physically, anyway — and I would often quietly mutter a simple thanks for having a job in which I wouldn't freeze in a bitter wind or suffer under a brutal sun or test a creaky back that had by then betrayed me.

I believe I work hard, harder than most folks who don't teach probably think I do; certainly harder than some of the folks at our state's Department of Education believe.

I recall a day even more years back than my coffee story when a teacher-farmer buddy of mine needed help with his hay. I told him I'd come down after school to help him throw a few loads into the loft before supper, and I met him, gloves stuffed into the back pocket of my blue jeans, just like they were when I was 16 and in need of gas money.

As we stood in the August heat summing up the courage to either be the one who tossed the bales on an ancient rusting hiker or the poor chump who'd arrange them lengthwise in the sauna of the barn, my friend's dad, a grizzled tiller of soil and chewer of tobacco, who had worked hard his whole life, walked up to us. He offered his help, but as was most often the case, he offered his opinion, too: Neither of us, he said, should be tired at all. We'd spent all day inside; that wasn't "real work," he added.

My friend nearly came out of his boots. "You don't have a clue, Dad," he said in a tone of voice that was as harsh as I'd ever heard him use with his father.

"I am more tired right now than if I had put up hay all day," he said, and he bit his lip and turned to throw a bale onto the hiker with deeper attention than was needed, I suppose so he wouldn't say anything else.

I think that is the case for most of us; no one, unless he's walked a mile or two in our boots or wingtips or heels or orthotics, understands what our job is truly about. Some of the hardest work I have ever faced was done behind a fast-food counter, in a grocery store aisle, or on a maintenance crew detail as a teenager or young, young man. I don't think anyone saw the "unskilled" tasks I handled as being "hard," but they were, and I was determined to do them well, whether it be cooking a hamburger or sweeping a floor or digging a post hole.

I have said it before in this space, and I'll say it again: We don't appreciate the work the average American laborer does anymore. We often want our children to grow up to wear white collars and striped ties and carry briefcases and make the big bucks, and that is admirable, but we have almost reduced getting dirty to being dirty, and I think that's too bad. Many of my heroes, my dad and my grandfathers, my mother and grandmothers, and a few of my good friends, too, never got college educations; some never finished high school. It was a different world in which they grew up, that is for sure, but one thing about them made me love and respect them all the more: They were never afraid to work for what they had, and they expected me to do the same.

This day, Labor Day, is for anyone who has ever waited tables, taken on the task of caring for ailing and elderly neighbors or parents, cleaned a house, or kept our electrical power on. It's for those who patch and plow our roads, trim our trees, dig our ditches, and watch our children. It's for those who take our blood pressure and stock our store shelves and deliver packages to our doors. It's for carpenters and teachers and store clerks and janitors, and it is for those who sit behind desks and clack on keyboards and man the phones. Labor Day is for those who work at their jobs and value their labor for more than a paycheck.

To me, Labor Day is a celebration of generations of hard work, not a recognition of my own life of earning a living. Like my family did years ago, I will stay home today to work at chores I can't usually get done during a regular work week. I won't be heading to a union rally or cheer on a speech, but I'll work a little, and I'll sweat a lot, and hopefully, I'll remember those folks who put me in a position to sit down when I want to.

Two dads whose gifts have never stopped coming
June 11, 2012

It is nearly a week until Father's Day, but I have had my dad, and my father-in-law — a second dad to me — on my mind today. I wrote about both men just a few weeks ago, but I have set my mind to write about them again anyway. I don't want this story to be sad; they both loved to laugh and wouldn't want that. No, I just wanted to tell them hello, and to thank them again for what they still do for me.

Many of us tend to believe that we quit giving things away when we die, that we had better get what we have to say said and our favorite belongings labeled and meted out before we make that one last trip to the graveyard. But I don't see it that way. My dad, Dan, has been gone for a decade and a half; my father-in-law, Gib, for a little more than three years. Yet, they continue to lend me a hand every so often, and I appreciate their help.

A few weeks back, on a very hot and very dry afternoon, I stopped in at my mother-in-law's place. I had decided that I had better get an old Seth Thomas mantel clock out of my father-in-law's cluttered little workshop, where I had taken it for Gib to fix just a few months before he died. He was not feeling well at the time, but he said he wanted to do it because he loved to tinker with clocks. Anyone can tell you that Gib could repair just about anything. It may have been with homemade parts, a bit of wire, a clump of solder, a mismatched screw, whatever he could come up with, but he'd get it to go.

I had bought the clock at auction — I have another that sits on my old office desk — not because they are very valuable, but because I love to hear them tick and chime.

But this particular clock, although in nice shape, had a broken pendulum, and there was no real way of telling if it still worked. So, knowing Gib was somewhat of a self-taught clocksmith, I took a gamble, paid a little more than I wanted to, and delivered it to him. I sat the clock on top of an old dresser in his shop, and he said he'd get to it when he got bored. Within days, he was in the hospital, and over the next few months, the clock sat in silence, gathered dust, and waited.

When I went to retrieve the piece, I was already mulling over the potential cost of getting it working again.

Clock repair isn't usually cheap. I even considered, briefly, searching the library and online for repair manuals, but I also knew from looking into the back of my working clock that we wouldn't get along. I recalled the time when I was about 10 years old and I tried to "repair" my brother's watch — I used a screwdriver and a tack hammer — but it didn't turn out well. And the watch wasn't even broken until I started working on it.

My truck in the drive, a door open, I walked into Gib's shop, picked up the clock and began to walk out with it under my arm. And it began to tick.

I sat it on the kitchen table, opened the back — a fist-sized tin cover that led the way to its inner workings — and saw the pendulum swinging in place. Within a minute or two, the clock chimed, and within an hour, I had it cleaned and wound. It has been ticking away on a cabin bookcase ever since...

A month or two after my dad suddenly passed years ago, my brother and brother-in-law and I reluctantly met to separate and share his tools. We made a nice toolbox for my mom to keep at home, for she always used a hodgepodge of mismatched screwdrivers and rusty pliers, and we thought she needed more than that. Three of the things I took home that day were a ladder, an old electric hand grinder, and an abused wheelbarrow that my dad had used for concrete work.

I found myself working at home late last week. I had what I call a "summertime grin" on my face, since I am away from school and can finally work on projects around my house and yard that I can't seem to get done when I have classroom work to tackle.

On that particular day, one in which the late spring heat had graciously taken vacation time and all I could hear were the mockingbirds and robins arguing between backyard trees, I decided that I was going to clean my gutters, work on a decrepit bird bath that had spent several years in solitary confinement in our barn, and build a stone flower bed near my cabin in which purple coneflower and brown-eyed Susans would be set to grow. It was after I had finished my first two jobs, and I had used the ladder to scale my roof and the grinder to remove a coat of rust from the birdbath, that I tackled the flower bed. It took much of the afternoon, but I hauled the stone and fill dirt from the piles I keep behind the barn, and I did it using the battered wheelbarrow that I had inherited.

Only when I was done, my hands still dripping from the scrubbing I had given them at our backyard hydrant, did I realize that I had used Dad's tools in all three jobs, and I silently told him, "Thanks, Pop."

This may be a bit early for Father's Day today, but I'll bet that most people reading it had, or have, a dad who has never stopped giving, whether they are living or not. I was lucky to have had two.

Wading deeper into the subject of Blue Herons
June 25, 2012

Like a relative who has worn out his welcome, the hot, parched weather of this young summer has already overstayed its visit with us, so my wife and I have found ourselves walking our road later in the evenings to keep our feet cool and our backs dry. In the smoldering mid-days of past weeks, we've hiked past waterless ditches and dusty fields, and even the birds we normally see have taken shelter to avoid the heat lamp of the sun. Now, we watch a later shift of wildlife checking in, including a Great Blue Heron we have seen standing in the dying evening light near the stagnant end of a withering pond.

Despite herons' having grown reputations as annoying raiders of suburban goldfish ponds, we admire these birds with their pole vault-like legs and sink trap-shaped necks, their scoliotic shoulders hunched in anticipation of finding a meal. Since we know not to speak loudly as we near the pond (primarily to avoid a neighborhood dog named Lug who loves to tag along on our walks), and the soles of our cushioned shoes make little noise on the pavement, we have been able to watch him a number of times as he stands in the shallows on his stilts, staring into the water like an old man remembering.

In time, he notices that he has an audience, so in a single, awkward lurch, he launches himself into a flight that appears improbable to us, that is until we see him get off the ground.

Great Blues (scientific name, *Ardea Herodias*, which literally means "heron" in both Latin and Greek) are big and interesting. Often nearing four-and-a-half feet from head to tail, they can have wingspreads as wide as 75 inches. Even though they appear to be an aerodynamic accident, they can recoil their long necks into their shoulders as they fly. Since their bones are hollow, herons often weigh only four to eight pounds, making their size deceptive, and they also have the distinction of owning knees that work in reverse, making their gait stilted and awkward.

The heron we watch has his pick of a half-dozen small neighborhood ponds, including the one that sits beneath the ridge on which our house is built. We have watched him fly over our place, only needing an occasional flap of his enormous wings as he catches the air on his trip west. We feel privileged that he has taken up residence near us, for herons have been spotted over a huge range of places, from coastal Alaska to Nova Scotia to Mexico. They've even been spotted in the Caribbean and in Europe, yet herons don't really migrate, often spending their entire 15-year lifespan in a relatively small place. Since we are homebodies, ourselves, I guess that is another reason why we like them.

Herons are wading birds, so unless we see one nesting or in mid-flight, we will find them near water. They love fish, but aren't finicky eaters, dining on frogs, aquatic insects, crawdads, even mice. In turn, because of their size, they don't have that many natural predators, although they do occasionally end up on the plate of a bobcat or coyote. Red-tailed hawks and bald eagles have also been known to get after them.

When we saw our heron earlier in the spring — and when we knew what regular rain felt like — he stood in clear, cool water well up onto the bank of a full pond. But now, he stands mostly in the weedy curling mud, straining to see his prey through a layer of tepid, lime-green scum. Nonetheless, we spy him in virtually the same spot each day, as if he has reserved a favorite table at a choice restaurant. In a way, we have used his legs as reedy yellow measuring sticks as the pond drops week after week in this lengthening drought.

We are hopeful that the Great Blue we watch has a nest nearby, which is likely. Herons usually re-use nests (the males are notorious rakes, often remodeling an old nest with a new mate), and they most often keep their own nest for several seasons. We're not certain that we are even seeing the same bird each time, for herons tend to live in colonies called "heronies," where parents share time sitting on three to five greenish-blue eggs. At eight weeks, the youngsters are pretty much on their own, but, like some college grads these days, young herons have been observed coming back to the nest for weeks afterward for a free meal and a warm place to stay.

Much of what I have read about herons involves how homeowners can get rid of them, for the birds do enjoy dining at backyard fountains, suburban ponds and urban spillways. It is not unusual to hear of people who use air horns and whistles and propane cannons to scare herons away; others use motion sensor lights, plastic alligators and firecrackers. Unfortunately, I also read of a study about blue herons and the devastating effects of industrial pollutants on them. It seems that although herons are big birds, they are very much at risk by what their human neighbors dump and discard and flush. It is no wonder they are seen as anti-social birds, rightfully earning the nickname, "Big Cranky."

Herons are solitary fellows; they don't seem to share the belief with most human beings that moving about and making noise are signs of progress. I guess the older that Joanie and I get to be, we agree with them. Maybe we're getting a bit cranky, too.

This summer has us recalling the heat of '36
July 9, 2012

It was "only" 99 degrees one afternoon last week when I decided to work on a backyard deck. With a jack and a drill and a little more sweat than I wanted to invest in the project, I went about the business of leveling its sags and dips a bit. The sun pounded down on my head and shoulders like a thug's blackjack, but as I packed my tools and drank a glass of cool water under a big maple tree a few hours later, I couldn't help but think about how lucky I've been these past few dusty and drought-stricken weeks.

I have worked under this summer's heat lamp for only a few hours at a time, but God help the roofers and utility linesmen and firemen, and so many others, who are out in it day after long hot day.

It's no news flash that the heat and lack of rain up and down the Wabash Valley have been brutal. Some of my farmer friends are worried that they may not have a bushel of beans or an ear of corn worth selling this fall; a few have already given up hope, and if you've seen their fields you know why. My yard, on which I refuse to waste water, is completely torched; it breaks and crunches under our feet as if we are walking on soda crackers. Despite our best efforts with both hose and watering can, we have already lost a few bushes and trees to a summer that, with the exception of 1988, may be the driest I can remember. I sound a bit like my grandfather when I say things like that. I keep writing about this drought with hopes that it in some way will help bring us rain, but so far, all I have managed are arid, empty words.

I quit washing the car with the optimism that it would surely bring us luck, mainly to conserve the water, and I have come to believe that when the weatherman says we have a 20-percent chance of rain, even he doesn't really believe it anymore.

My old air conditioning unit has had a rough time keeping up with the temperature readings this past month too, and by the early evening our house is a little warmer than we want it to be. I always give its coils a good cleaning in the spring before the hot months arrive, but this year's temperatures have just about brought it to its knees. Of course, we're fortunate to have it. When I was a boy, I couldn't have known then what a difference it makes to sleep in an air-conditioned house, but I sure know it now. I remember waking up years ago to the drone of the cicadas coming through our screened windows, sometimes before the sun was even up, knowing that it was going to be a bare-footed and shirtless kind of day best spent under a front yard beech tree.

We can't help ourselves, I suppose, in comparing this blast furnace of a June and July (please remember that we have August ahead of us too) to other wicked summers. We are setting heat records this year, and many of the new marks are topping those from the mid-30s, particularly 1936. In my childhood summers, I remember sitting in front of a whispering and rotating black metal fan with my grandpa, who never wore short pants, but often stripped down to an undershirt when it went above 90 degrees. I know I asked him how he withstood the heat in the days before he could afford even that wheezing old fan.

My grandfather was 34 years old in 1936; by that time he was working on WPA (Works Progress Administration) road and pipeline projects. He told me that he dug ditches one shovel of dry dirt at a time, and he also spent his days applying hot tar to the joints of smoldering iron pipes that were too hot to touch. It made me sweat to even think about his doing that, and it made me realize, even when I was 12 or 13 years old, and quite indestructible, that he was made of stouter stuff than I was. He could stand out in that kind of sun and hoe beans or pull sweet corn long after I sought back porch shade and a cold, sweating bottle of Pepsi.

My dad, who was only six in that dreaded summer, told me that even in milder summers their house was too stifling to sleep and eat in, so my grandparents often took him and my Aunt Elenore out onto the porch or the lawn for meals and bedtime. He said they went to the creek every day in an attempt to wash and cool off, but that by mid-July the trickling stream that ran under the Harry Evans Bridge was as warm as "bath water." Because of those days, I suppose, he never became very dependent on air conditioning. I remember he would run it on the hottest days in his work truck, but kept his windows rolled down anyway.

When it seems as though the collective pain of the Great Depression could not have made people much more miserable, the weather in the middle of the decade conspired to do just that. A record-cold February, and a tornado-ridden April, were followed by a season of tortuous heat. Record July highs had already been set in 1931, 1933, and 1934, so folks had been used to hot summers, yet 1936 topped them all. From a story written just a year ago by the Tribune-Star's Lisa Trigg, I learned that highs of 98 degrees on July 2 and July 4 of 1936 seemed to be just the beginning. By July 7, my dad's birthday, it was 107 in Terre Haute, making it the "hottest place in the Midwest." The street temperature that day was measured at 122 degrees on the downtown concrete.

By July 12, Terre Haute registered 108 degrees and the killer heat was on a roll; nearly 1,200 people had died in the Midwest by then, but the toll would eventually be much higher. By July 14, it was 110 degrees in Terre Haute, a record that no one was celebrating. Residents of Collegeville, near Rensselaer, to our north, were hardly celebrating either: It was 116 degrees there, setting a record for Indiana that has never been topped.

The summer of '36 beat on the nation well into August. Spotty rains alleviated the drought in some areas, while others remained parched and dry. On July 25 — my mom's second birthday — 3.37 inches of rain fell on Terre Haute; by 7 that evening, it was back up to 90 degrees; it rose to 102 the next day. By mid-August another cruel, 11-day heat wave hit the Midwest.

I watered a few flowers behind the house in the early evening after my deck work that day, and as I did I watched a gray bank of clouds build to the southwest of us. I decided to take a walk despite what appeared to be the threat of a storm, but as I leaned into the cooling wind, I smelled no rain in the air. I spotted only one solitary dragonfly as he flew patrol over a baked and thirsty soybean field, and even the weeds in the ditches looked yellow and tired. As I passed a neighbor's house, I saw a friend rinsing off the plastic blades of a fan with a garden hose.

"Looks like we're going to finally get some rain," she said to me with an optimistic smile. Unfortunately, we didn't get a drop, and just as it was in 1936, we'll just have to wait.

Thoughts on smooth stones and blue water
July 23, 2012

It was raining when I began to write this. Although no one could rightfully call what we got this afternoon a "downpour," it was nice to have my windows open to hear the steady drops of a passing shower tapping on my dry-as-dust deck and hard-as-concrete yard. For some reason, the old weather junker we've been trying to jump-start for months decided to turn over and run a little while, and we were thankful for even the tenth of an inch or so that my grass soaked up like a sponge.

We are back after being away for a few days to our favorite place on Lake Michigan. It was hard to leave the beach to return here to our arid yards and withered trees, for we sat in the sand and sun and listened to nothing man-made for hours on end. It soon became hard for us to even remember such dry ground as ours when all we could hear was the constant lapping of the lake's blue-green waves as they just kept coming and coming and coming at us.

Since my kids are no longer kids, and their work schedules and busy lives now rule the whens and wheres of our trips together, we have fallen into the pleasant habit of visiting the great lake together for a little while instead of planning longer vacations. We like it there because it is quiet and uncrowded, and there isn't a shopping mall within reasonable driving distance. Thankfully, none of us, my new daughter-in-law included, wanted to see asphalt parking lots or amusement rides, check-out lines or continental breakfasts. We ate in small, locally owned restaurants, thumbed through a few antique shops, and took walks in the evenings, but always it was the lake and its endless shore that called to us, morning, afternoon, and evening.

Unlike last year when we encountered all kinds of mechanical obstacles to get there, and we all baked in the parking lot of a tire and brake shop along the way, we had no trouble in reaching the lake this time around. For a while, the traffic was mean and hurried, but once we shed the interstates we saw more cornfields than cars. It was 97 degrees when we pulled off the highway for good, and 20 degrees cooler than that when we reached the bottom of the long stairway that took us out to the beach on that first late afternoon. Southern Michigan, like central Indiana, is dry, although I got the sense that folks there have had a little more rain than we have had, which isn't hard since we haven't had a decent spit come our way for over two months now.

Seeing the marram grass and the shorebirds and feeling the grit of the sand between our toes for the first time in a year was like finding a favorite cousin at a yearly reunion. We quickly made ourselves at home on the beach, each seeing something different on that far blue horizon, the wind making Brillo pads of our hair and reddening our faces. For most part, all conversations stopped...

I am a bit of a rock hound from years back, and even though I have picked up and packed off a ton of Lake Michigan's sand-smoothed gray-black basalt over the years, I told my wife that I wanted to collect a few of the more colorful beach stones for our aquarium at home. So, on that first full morning on the lake, she promptly emptied a large plastic zip-top bag and told me to knock myself out. She was soon stretched out in a lounge chair, a towel for a pillow, a beach umbrella over her head, and a new whodunit on her lap, and rightfully so. Like the watchful mom she is, I know that she occasionally glanced up to make sure that neither I nor her kids, had disappeared in the rip tides, but otherwise she tackled her book, while I walked and picked and discarded and kept what interested me.

By our last day on the beach, I had not only acquired a bit of a sunburn, for as I usually do—I had underestimated the amount of lotion that I needed — but an impressive collection of granites and quartzes and cherts, none longer than the pocket knife I carry in my blue jeans.

I found feldspars (often called "moonstone") and small geodes (none large enough to crack), and even a few pieces of "Lightning Stone," which is actually siderite spidered with calcite veins. I was quite proud of myself.

To be honest, I had a few stones that I couldn't identify at all, so I turned to an article by Kathi Mirto when I returned home. She is a Michigan rock hunter who posts nice photos of and articles about Lake Michigan on the web. From her description, I think I also picked up a piece of septarium, a reddish-brown bedrock that, like Lightning Stone, is veined with calcite. Mirto writes: "Another name for [septarium] sometimes is Turtle Stone, obviously due to [its] resemblance of a turtle shell pattern. Sand-smoothed granite and limestone are other common stones found nearby the brown stones. The deep gray and other various colored stones provide a striking contrast from the warm reddish-brown tones."

Before we left the lake, we hurriedly packed our bags and quickly loaded the family wagon so we could spend a little time on the beach before we turned our backs on it for home. There was just a hint of a breeze that morning and the lake was as calm as I have ever seen it. Joanie and my daughter, Ellen, and I walked down to the water's edge, not wanting to leave at all, but if a half-an-hour was all we had left, we decided to spend it the way we wanted. I began to look for stones.

In the clear shallows of that serene July morning, I picked up rocks that looked as if they'd come from a jeweler's tumbler. I found tiny crinoids and corals, too small to have been seen when the waves were rough, and I pocketed two pieces of polished glass, made milky and dull by the countless times they'd rolled across the sands of the lakebed. I filled my pockets.

As we were about to leave that morning, we noticed that a child had written, "Bye" in a ridge of sand that faced the lake. In my mind, I added, "See you next year..."

Summer's hidden beauty worth the wait
August 20, 2012

The great naturalist John Burroughs once said that nature teaches more than she preaches. I can't recall a summer where that rings true more than this one, for that old sun of ours truly taught us a thing or two these past three months.

It has been a brown season, a year of the withered and seared and thirsty, and it isn't just because we now have a new roof on our house that I am hopeful for a wet, cool fall. Due to the recent rains, the landscape we see from our windows is a little less tired and worn than it was just a week ago, but we still hope our trees can soon prop their feet up to rest and store autumn color. I am descended from the English and the Welsh, so I think it's my genetic disposition to hope for rain and mist and soggy ground. Yet, amid the realities of costlier food and lower wells and the depressing ugliness of scruffy weeds and scorched fields, I have been surprised by another of nature's lessons: In the driest of years there remains beauty and color and life, even if it does barely survive under an umbrella of toasted leaves or grovels in the cracked earth of a ditch that last ran full in March.

In just the past few days, I have scribbled a rather impressive list of the living things I have spied among the dead and dying. Our tall friend, the blue heron I wrote about a month or so ago, stood a good while and looked us over as we walked past the tepid pond he had staked out a few Sundays back. It was as if he had taken a number and was waiting for a turn in a line he didn't want to abandon, so he just kept a wary eye on us as we sauntered by. We must be becoming friends, for I caught him fishing in our garden bird bath one day last week, too. An oriole, perhaps an acquaintance of his, flitted past me that same day. He provided a pleasant flash of orange and black that stood out in stark contrast to a field of crunchy brown clover, as do the lightning-quick goldfinches who go after our fading coneflowers.

It had already proven to be a field day of sorts, for I had stopped my truck in the road only a few hours earlier to move a big box turtle as he hot-footed it from ditch to ditch. With his long yellow neck extended, he, too, stared at me, all the while treading the air until I set him down in a patch of crunchy weeds. He went about his business without offering his thanks, but since it had been months since I had even seen a turtle, I didn't mind his rudeness.

One of the few positives of our baked earth is that the moles have given up digging in my yard for a while. I can just see them with bruised snouts as they wait for hearty fall rains like the rest of us. Our bees, however, wait for nothing. Even as I last watered our garden's coneflowers and day lilies and sedum, they buzzed in and out of the hose's shower, enjoying the bath as they gathered and transported pollen. The wasps keep trying to build under my back porch door light, and it appears as though it has been a banner year for those big burrowing ground hornets, the B-52s of the insect world, for they are drilling and digging away near my garage like wildcatters in an Oklahoma oil field.

We have also lately been visited by a gregarious praying mantis. My wife has watched him as he travels from one of our hummingbird feeders to another. Whether he likes the nectar or the ants who steal sips for themselves is yet to be determined, but his brashness seems to be wearing thin on the birds that hum about him. Joanie has had to brush him onto a porch railing as she fills the feeders, but before long he is arrogantly back to his perch.

We have had encounters with horseflies and grasshoppers and crickets lately, as well, but it is the swallowtail butterflies that are breaking up the monotony of our brown landscape the most. They enjoy the marigolds near my cabin, but they have to share the area with a furtive little skink that slips between and under the rock wall I built there.

Despite the lack of moisture, there is surprising life in the weed patches and fence rows and fields we wander past. Of course, we always hear and see the killdeer and the rabbits and the sparrows, and about dusk, we watch bats dipping and diving in the dying light. Just the other day, we found a big dragonfly droning away near the road, his deep blues and greens a real treat. There are wildflowers and weeds making it among the frail and the dead, too. For instance, we have watched a decent crop of field thistle mature along the roadway, its anemone-like purple blooms bursting from big thorny heads. Daisy-like fleabane and purple pokeweed prosper nearby, and if we look for it, we can always find thin sprigs of yellow sweet clover growing. Its tiny blooms smell like a new-mown hayfield when crushed between our fingers.

There are purplish-blue bits of rogue alfalfa growing in the ditches, too, and despite there being nothing all summer but a little morning dew to water it, bright blue lettuce and purple clover continued to bloom. So did the graceful Queen Anne's Lace that, year after year, despite frequent mowing and dry stretches and herbicides, just keeps coming back. We have also discovered a stand of evening primrose, which this year grows alone while the grasses that normally obscure it bow at its feet, the nasty sun and dry wind beating them into submission long ago.

Despite it being intertwined with a healthy clump of poison ivy, which never seems to have a bad year, a stand of honeysuckle still blooms; Joanie and I smell it before we ever see it. Each night, as we walk by, I snatch a tendril of the stuff, and without missing a step, we take turns inhaling its perfume before we drop it to head on up the road to become observers of windblown foxtail and the sturdy spikes of yellow wooly mullein. We also have watched the Johnson grass mature. A "noxious" pest to farmers, it is, nonetheless, a pretty plant, and now, despite the heat, has formed a russet-colored flower head that will soon drop its seeds.

Just a few nights ago, as I stood in our back yard and despaired at my bristled brown grass and the condition of a wild cherry tree that may have been just days away from dying of thirst, I spotted a woodpecker as he landed on the limb of a sycamore tree not 30 feet away. Showy, and as big as a crow, he was apparently in no mood to make friends, for he soon flew deeper into the woods and out of sight.

I waited a while, hoping he'd come back to give me another look at his dramatic red and black and white jacket and his long beak, but he never did. Like much of the beauty I have discovered this summer, I had to look hard and wait long. It has been worth the trouble.

The 'devil's coachman' in our yard
September 17, 2012

I've had a good time opening my mail these past few weeks. Sure, I still received the usual junk about lower credit card rates and satellite television packages, but the genuine letters made me smile; most were about a story I wrote in late August.

That column was about the "hidden beauty" of our drought-stricken summer, and in it I mentioned a praying mantis that had taken up residence on one of our hummingbird feeders. With that revelation going public, my readers took pen in hand, or in some cases, pulled their chairs up to a computer keyboard. But, one way or the other, they got their letters to me, and for that reason alone, I just had to read more about "mantids" and why people find them so interesting.

We have always had an abundance of praying mantises on our property, which is to my understanding, a good sign, both literally and figuratively. We have large hedges at the northernmost corners of our house, and I have seen mantises making their way through and over them like mountain climbers, silently complaining, I suppose, that the racket of my mower and weed whacker was interrupting their quests in search of a meal. Mantids have always been touted as beneficial insects, and it is true that they eat many garden pests like aphids and gnats, even the moths who leave their disgusting and hungry larvae on my shrubs.

In reality, however, praying mantises are gluttonous, voracious eating machines that consume just about anything they can catch, including the gentle and beautiful and pollinating insects who often become snack food before they can produce proper non-pest ID.

Nearly every letter writer wanted me to know that the mantis my wife had been scooting off her feeders in the evenings wasn't there to share a slurp of sugar water with our hummingbirds. It was there, in all probability, to snare and eat a bird, something that I wouldn't have believed had I not subsequently seen so much literature on the subject, even watched a rather gruesome home video of such an assault that the faint-of-heart should avoid it.

Emailer Norma Plasack wrote, "It might be a good idea to take your praying mantis for a walk into the woods and hope he doesn't find his way back." So, we did just that, but since we didn't take prints or mugshots, we had no way of knowing if the mantis my wife found on the same feeder a few days later was the same one we had carted off.

I also received a note from a writer who identified herself only as Elizabeth. She wrote: "When I saw your photo of the praying mantis on the hummingbird feeder, it reminded me of how excited I was to have one on my hummingbird feeder last summer. I also took a good photo of it. Since then, 'Birds and Blooms' magazine has informed us that the praying mantis is a hummingbird predator!"

"Birds and Blooms" must have a circulation that rivals "Time" because I heard from a whole host of other folks who had read the same story. Pat Fash, one of my Illinois readers, said she discovered a mantis eating a hummer on one of her feeders. After brushing it away, she found the same mantis on the feeder the very next day, so Pat's husband was forced to do what he had to do...

There are actually three species of praying mantises in the Midwest, and about 2,000 species worldwide. According to Purdue entomologist Tom Turpin, there are about 20 species in the United States. The clan that has staked out a homestead on our place could be a European (*Mantis religiosa*), a Chinese (*Tenodera aridifolia*), or a Carolina mantis (*Stagmomantis Carolina*). Considering its considerable size, our friend was probably both female and of the Chinese variety, although I doubt whether it will ever grow to rival the largest-known mantis that was spotted in southern China in 1929. It was measured at 18 inches in length, which I don't mind saying, sends a shiver up my spine and vaguely reminds me of an old science fiction movie I watched on the "Early Show" years ago.

The word "mantis" originated with the Greeks; it literally means "diviner" or "fortune-teller." For that rather mystic reason, praying mantises seem to be steeped in folklore. In an article printed about a year ago by Carol Michel, the author quotes William Atherton Dupuy, whose "Insect Friends and Foes" was first printed in 1925. Dupuy wrote that the English came to call mantises "soothsayers," and that many old-timers believed that the direction of a pointing mantis could lead lost children back home. It was also believed that young French women looked for mantises to point out the places from which their lovers would come.

In the scientific world, the praying mantis is an interesting study. Equipped with a head that can rotate 180 degrees, it can see and hear exceedingly well, while its antennae are "most likely used for smell." Mantids do primarily eat insects, but they are arrogant enough to believe that the occasional frog or small mammal is fair game, too. In turn, bats, snakes, birds and large frogs are more than willing to dine on mantises. If that doesn't happen, they cannibalize their own kind — which often happens to male mantises just after mating with the larger, more physical females. They really aren't very finicky eaters at all. As friend Deanna Sinclair wrote in her letter to me, "When the mantises mate, it is a short honeymoon. The female bites the head off her mate."

Our nights are getting cooler now; fall is in the air and creeping ever so closer on our calendars. In years when the winters are very mild, mantises have been known to live quite a while, but, for most part, they lay their eggs (which overwinter under a stem or leaf), and succumb to the cold and frost. So, not long after our hummingbirds have put up the storm windows, packed their bags and taken off for the Yucatan, our mantises are already counting their days. Some mantises can, in fact, fly, but they're built for local commutes only.

It is said that just sighting a praying mantis is a sign of good luck. If that is the case, we have been blessed many times this summer. In folklore, the praying mantis has also been called a "rearhorse," a "mule killer," and "the devil's coachman," the latter epithet used because they appear to be holding the reins of a horse-drawn carriage.

We'll look for mantises on our feeders next year, but I want to tell them right now: We know exactly what they're up to.

Mice really do play when the cat's away
July 8, 2013

I am rarely away from my place much in the summer. I like the quiet here and don't yearn to be gone for very long at a time. To me, a vacation often means that I don't have to start my car for days on end, or put on socks, for that matter. But this year has been different; my wife and I took a two-week driving trip through New England, the longest vacation we've ever had without our kids along for the ride. We had a great time, but when we got back, we were surprised to learn that all kinds of things had been going on in our absence.

I'm not talking about a break-in or a wild party. The place was locked up tight, frequently checked on, even lived in a while as the two of us hit the hottest spots in Maine and Vermont, that is if you like the homes of poets, coastline walking trails and moose rehabilitation centers.

No, the changes in and around our house were subtle, little things that made me realize that my yard and my gardens, even unused rooms, change when no one is there to walk through them.

We saw proof of this observation first-hand before we ever returned home: The last stop on our tour was Steepletop, poet Edna St. Vincent Millay's home until her death in 1950. The farm, comprised mostly of woods and rolling hillsides, is near Austerlitz, New York. Millay's place stood empty for more than a decade, that coming after her sister, who moved in to preserve her famous sibling's possessions, passed away. In just 10 years of vacancy, most of the time and labor and money that Millay had invested in turning the farmstead into a showplace (it had 13 inter-locking gardens and a magnificent pool and rock walls) became unapparent. It will take the Edna St. Vincent Millay Society hundreds of thousands of dollars and many years to restore the place; we'd love to go back to see it when the work is completed.

Joanie and I arrived home from our trip very late after driving all day across three states. I could tell as the headlights of our car swept across the driveway that night that the weeds I occasionally pick out of the white rock on my way to the barn or mailbox had gone unchecked; I couldn't believe that I could see them, in some instances three or four inches tall, growing in places that were barren just a few weeks before. I made a mental note to get after them the very next morning.

Before we ever went to bed, we saw even more proof of how quickly an unoccupied home can go into decline. We had turned our air conditioning up to save a bit of energy while we were gone, so the house was warm and musty. That was remedied quickly enough, but it hadn't been 20 minutes after I brought in the last load of vacation gear from the trunk that I heard Joanie voice her displeasure — rather loudly and in a higher pitch than usual — over spotting a mouse in our kitchen. It had come out of an open utility closet door, taken a good look at the strange creature standing at the kitchen sink, then ran for the security of the crack between a cabinet and our refrigerator.

We haven't seen a mouse, even evidence of one, in our house for years, but it was obvious to us that night why we were seeing one then. Not only had the place been very quiet in our absence, but we also had boarded our housecat, a three-year-old neurotic named Edgar, at our local veterinarian, so he'd have steady doses of food and attention. We were actually afraid he'd destroy our house while we were gone... Edgar enjoys shredding our hands and arms after his purrs lull us into patting him, but it is now obvious that he — and his predecessor, Arthur — must have been a pretty good rodent-deterrent system for us. Joanie was picking up Edgar the next day, so we set a trap near the refrigerator and went to bed.

A few years ago, I read Alan Weisman's "The World Without Us," in which the author used all sorts of scientific data to paint a picture of what this planet would be like if people were no longer walking on it. In some instances, Weisman depicted the minor but certain changes that would be seen in as little as two weeks or so. Images from his book came to mind as I walked my yard that first morning of our return.

Although my son had mowed the yard in my absence, I still found the usual litter strewn in the grass, both fallen from my trees and tossed from passing cars. I also discovered that huge black ants had taken up residence in the big patio umbrella I'd laid on our deck to keep the wind from blowing it open. They had already furiously built quite a metropolis for themselves, tending to and doting over a host of big yellow-white eggs. I shook them out and got the umbrella back up.

I also soon noticed that everything had grown, not just my grass, but the corn and soybeans in nearby fields. I mean REALLY grown — perhaps a foot or more in the heat of a humid June. A golden raintree sapling that I had started in my garden, and am going to transplant soon, had shot up another six inches or more in the time we were gone, as had my tomato plants and hollyhocks. I began pulling weeds and creepers away from flower beds that were clean just a few weeks before; I couldn't imagine what a month's absence would do to my place if I were not around to tend to it.

The moles had gone crazy in my absence, too. Without my vigilance, they took it upon themselves to tunnel themselves silly — huge mounds of yellow-red clay signaling the approach to their city of destruction near a trio of blue spruce trees on the north edge of the property. The wasps had built nice-sized nests under my cabin door and along a back porch gutter; I wasn't home to swat them away. Just about everywhere I looked, coneflowers had bloomed, hostas had sprouted purple, and sunflowers had tripled in size. My sole grapevine was nearly covered over by a purplish-green invasive that I don't even know by name, and Joanie and I both walked through cobwebs — contorting and spitting as we went through our garage. I found new spider webs in my cabin, too, spun from books to windows, doors to lamps.

We also gained two freeloaders that we're not particularly happy about, both creating havoc and intimidation without us there to nip it in the bud. A raccoon has clearly been taking advantage of our absence by raiding bird feeders for seed and nectar, and a brutish gray-and-white tomcat — quite the thug — has made himself at home around the place, bullying our old barn cat, Max, and stealing every morsel of food he can find. Their fates are yet to be determined...

We've been home long enough now that things have pretty well returned to normal. The recent monsoons are the only thing keeping me from my duties as groundskeeper, but the shrubs are trimmed and the house de-funked. The moles and ants and unruly vines have been whipped into shape whether they like it or not.

The mouse, I am happy to say, has been dispatched, not by Edgar, but by deception, a bit of Colby Jack cheese, and a trap. After a few weeks away from home, Edgar now expects his meals in bed.

'Whose woods these are, I think I know...'
July 21, 2013

A few summers ago, my family traveled to New England to see what we could see. Along the way, we dipped our toes into Walden Pond, holy waters to those who have read Henry David Thoreau. My wife and I returned to the region last month to seek shrines that poets at heart revere: The Vermont homes where Robert Frost wrote magical words.

Our drive into southern Vermont was relaxed and winding, and we skirted the growing ridges of the Green Mountains, cruising much of the way alongside a rain-fed and rocky stream called Roaring Branch. We had left the interstate a few miles out of Massachusetts, and drove two-lane Highway 9 all the way to Bennington. There, we found Frost's grave in the magnificent Old First Church cemetery, dotted with tall slender grave markers of Revolutionary War veterans, most of which that carried engravings of death's heads, weeping willows, and inverted torches. Frost's grave, to the east and down a slope from the back of the church, is found in a simple plot. A white birch tree — an important symbol to the poet — and a view of the mountains only partially explain why Frost chose a gravesite for his family in a place in which he'd never lived.

After his wife, Elinor, died in 1938, Frost had originally planned to scatter her ashes on a farm he had owned near Derry, New Hampshire, a place we had to save for another trip to New England. When he returned to the old farm there, its owners were not enthused about the poet's plan; the farm's state of disrepair also bothered him. Instead, Frost waited two more years before deciding to create a family plot in Bennington, just a few miles south of another of his homes in Shaftsbury.

It was early evening before we left the cemetery and the growing shadows cast by its maple leaves for another nice but twisting drive up Highway 7 to Manchester, where we would stay the night in a lodge that gave us a misty morning view of the mountains. It was hard to explain, but neither of us was in a hurry to leave the old poet's grave. He outlived not only his wife by a quarter of a century, but four of his five children (all are buried alongside him) and so we felt a bit sad. His famous line, "I had a lover's quarrel with the world," serves as his epitaph.

Our visit to Frost's "Stone House" in Shaftsbury began the next morning, a day on which the sun was hazed by skirting clouds. Frost lived on the farm from 1920-1929, planting scores of apple and pine trees, and writing many of the poems — including "Stopping by Woods on a Snowy Evening" — that were included in his first Pulitzer Prize-winning collection, "New Hampshire." Built in 1769, the house sits just yards from the busy two-lane highway, which was a simple gravel road in the poet's tenure there. The house's stone walls are nearly two feet thick, so when we entered the place through its back door it was cool and quiet. The few other visitors who came and went quietly walked the broad pine floor planks with little comment.

As much as I enjoyed the inside of the house (we were allowed to wander through only a few downstairs rooms, but learned much about Frost), it was the yard and paths near the house I enjoyed most. A long stone wall stretched itself to the west of a small barn, and a mowed

162

path took me back to an apple tree that appeared vigorously healthy from a distance, but was remarkably hollow when I got close enough to get a better look.

Walking the pasture gave me a sense of where the poet wandered and what he saw from his back door. I imagine he added a few stones to the wall and sat in a high-backed chair under the birch and maple trees along his driveway. It proved, however, to be a poor decision on my part to walk a while on the paths behind the house in shorts; the chiggers and black flies got the best of me, but the welts they left on my arms and ankles were still worth the trip.

It was a longer drive northward, out of, but then back into the mountains, toward Ripton, where Frost bought yet another farm in the summer after Elinor died. Unable to live alone without his wife, and nearly debilitated by his grief, Frost moved back to Shafstbury to live with his son for a while. But after a lecture at the Bread Loaf Writer's Conference, Frost decided to purchase the Homer Noble farm, not far from Ripton on scenic Highway 125. The simple farmhouse, which sits at the end of a long and steep gravel lane, had a cabin behind it. Friends Kay and Ted Morrison eventually lived in the house, Kay taking on Elinor's duties as a secretary of sorts to Frost. The Morrisons, and their two children and dogs lived in the house, while Frost stayed in the cabin; he did take many of his meals with the family.

Not knowing that the farm was just a stone's throw

away, we first stopped at the Robert Frost Trail to stretch our legs and heads a bit. It is a beautiful place, well maintained by the Green Mountain National Forest and dotted with markers bearing Frost's words. It was an easy walk of less than a mile-and-a-half, and we passed over a bridge that spanned a fork of the Middlebury River, not far from a marsh that beavers and dragonflies call home. After a green-canopied and pine-scented hike, we reached several clearings dominated by blueberry and huckleberry bushes, and bird boxes. At about the time we headed back into the forest to meet up with the bridge again, we caught a glimpse of Frost's farmhouse roof peaking above the trees to the north, so we knew where we'd be headed next.

As had become customary for this trip, Joanie and I made our way to the farm and the cabin late in the day. When we pulled up in front of the house, we could tell that no one was there, and it was unlikely that anyone would bother us. A sign on the door of the house told us that we could tour the grounds as long as we wished, and that we should simply leave things as they are. It is remarkable trust, considering that the cabin was vandalized just a few years ago.

We stayed in Frost's yard for nearly two hours, but only near the house for a little while before we found the path that headed even further up the same slope past rock walls to the cabin, which is nestled under sugar maples at the edge of the woods. Later, we both swore we could feel the old poet lingering there, particularly, I think, as we sat on a cairn of granite that he surely sat upon too, looking southward to an orchard grass meadow and the mountains beyond. We each sat in that spot a long time, silent, taking notes and thinking thoughts, but mostly appreciating that we were able to make the visit.

We became inspectors of everything that we thought Frost had a hand in — the blackberry bushes and apple trees halfway down the hill, the bookcases and bathtub that we could spy through the cabin windows, the woodshed, now empty.

Eventually, we reluctantly walked down the hill, not wanting to leave the cabin behind, but instead of driving away, we sat again, this time on huge boulders near the drive, listening to no more than the ravings of a red-winged blackbird who thought we needed to go.

I fail miserably at memorizing poetry, but I do recall that Frost wrote a poem about leaving his 30-acre farm in Derry, which he sold in 1911 to finance his family's move to England. It ends with these lines:

> *"It shall be no trespassing*
> *If I come again some spring*
> *In the grey disguise of years,*
> *Seeking ache of memory here."*

Perhaps, some spring, or summer, we will come back to this place, no doubt a little greyer, seeking our own memories...

'Once more to the lake'

July 22, 2013

Union Pier, Mich. — We are heading home today after spending a few days on Lake Michigan, and I am a bit sad for the leaving. We have made it a habit to come here every year, dragging weary bones and beach towels and enough breakfast food to last us a week. And, as expected, when I turn my back on the cool blueness of the lake for the last time this afternoon, I'll know that another year has gone by, and there's no getting it back.

I spent one evening alone on this trip, sitting on the beach and reading from a short stack of books. My wife and daughter, and my son, with his fairly new wife in tow, were off to other places that night while I chose solitude, a soft western breeze, and the sound of lapping waves until it was nearly too dark to see my way back up the long stairway from the sand to our cabin's front porch light.

As is often the case, one of the books I had with me was a collection of essays by E.B. White; it seems as though I re-read him in the summers, and on a whim I had shoved the book into my backpack with a notepad and ink pen, a guide to Lake Michigan's geology, and a new history of the Normandy invasion that I knew I'd finish before our days on the lake were to end.

In the fading light, and with the protests of spatting gulls in my ears, I stabbed both thumbs into the book, willing to read the first essay that came up, and as luck would have it — or simply because the book now just falls open to the spot — White's "Once More to the Lake" stared back at me.

White wrote the essay in August 1941, and it remains one of my favorites. Just a little over seven pages, "Once More..." is his account of staying on a lake in Maine each August as a boy with his family, beginning in 1904. Years later, a successful writing career well under way, a family of his own, and a life on a "salt-water farm" on the coast, had not dimmed White's memories.

He wrote: "I have since become a salt-water man, but sometimes in the summer there are days when the restlessness of the tides and the fearful cold of the sea water and the incessant wind that blows across the afternoon and into the evening make me wish for the placidity of a lake in the woods. A few weeks ago this feeling got so strong I bought myself a couple of bass hooks and a spinner and returned to the lake where we used to go, for a week's fishing and to revisit old haunts."

I know it may take a leap of faith to make those words relate to our family visits to Lake Michigan, for like White's Atlantic breezes and relentless tides, the lake in which we wade here is more akin to an ocean than a quiet and still country pool. At the latter, the sponginess of moss between your toes, the scent of stagnant shallows and rotting cattails, and the slimy feel of a bass in your hands overwhelm the senses. Not so, on the Great Lake, with its constant wind whistling through the marram grass, its sand pails and beach umbrellas, its roaring waves.

No, the real connection between White's return to his Maine lake and my run up interstate highways to the loud slapping waters of Lake Michigan comes in more of a nostalgic sense. White wrote the essay after he'd taken his son to the lake, and in doing so, he relived the sights and sounds and feels of the experience as both a boy and as an aging father who watches his son fish and swim and marvel at dragonflies. He sees the passage of time, and how quickly a life can come and go. As he put it: "It seemed to me, as I kept remembering all this, that those times and those summers had been infinitely precious and worth saving. There had been jollity and peace and goodness."

So, too, it is with me. We have been traveling north to the lake for years now, really to do nothing but walk the beach and collect smooth stones and to bury our feet in the sand. We sleep in the sun and watch the horizon and read good books. We drink deeply from the needed rest, and like White, we store away the memories as he did of his dad who once rolled a canoe in the lake, of the tarred road that led to the cabins, and of the "sleepy sound" of the little outboard motors on their boats.

In the long run, I think I most appreciate the simple power of White's words. Yes, he wrote beloved children's classics, and it is right and well that he should be remembered for them. But for me, it is his essays that speak more loudly, more significantly.

"I kept remembering everything," he wrote near the end of the piece. "After breakfast we would go up to the store and the things were in the same place — the minnows in a bottle, the plugs and spinners disarranged and pawed over by the youngsters from the boys' camp, the Fig Newtons and the Beeman's gum. ... Everywhere we went I had trouble making out which was I, the one walking at my side, the one walking in my pants."

If we are lucky, we have places that we can go to, and return to, times over. Places where the familiar things are good to us, that remind us how lucky we are, like a glassy lake in Maine, like a rolling bluegreen, fresh-water sea in Michigan. I'm sure that when White left his lake to return to the Maine coast, even back to his smoky office at "The New Yorker," he was happy to be home, like we will be when we pull into our driveway tonight on our return to Parke County and its cornfields.

It is odd that today, of all times, I remember E.B. White's words. Just last month, my wife and I drove all the way to Brooklin, Maine, to try to visit that salt-water farm of his. We drove the same roads he drove, walked the same library he walked, spoke to a few folks who knew him. But today, I think I understood him, and that may be worth even more.

Mike Lunsford

-Fall -

"Another fall, another turned page: there was something of
jubilee in that annual autumnal beginning, as if last year's
mistakes had been wiped clean by summer."

Wallace Stegner

Fall's arrival heralded in
ever-present fencerows

September 19, 2011

As much as I hate summer to leave us, I am happy
that fall is just around the corner. It has been a bone-dry
season, one in which I've watched my yard bake and crack
like an old pie crust. My wife and I are still spending our
evenings going about the business of watering flowers,
standing with a dribbling hose in our hands, optimistically
hoping that our drought will be broken because we've
tempted the weather fates to do us one better and give us a
good rain.

As has been my habit, I am walking my road in the
cool of the evenings, and I've begun to notice that the
fencerows and fields and trees are changing their colors for
autumn, not unlike those of us who will soon be
scrounging in the closet for a favorite sweater or faded
flannel shirt to slip on. I have always been interested in
fencerows, and before you think that I need to desperately
seek a real hobby, I'll tell you why.

It has been suggested that fencerows, no matter
how unkempt and ragged, create a boundary between

171

what we know and what we don't. They divide the land — perhaps segregate that which is neatly kept from that which isn't — and they create barriers between what is ours and what is someone else's. But more than that, I am interested in what lives in or near fencerows. Not the horses and cattle kept away from the roads and orchards by wire strung along dried and graying posts, but rather the insects and birds, the ivies and creepers and snakes that make the fencerows their home. Spray as one will, or mow, or scythe, and sooner or later fencerows will fill themselves with vines and burrows and buzzes that survive in few other places.

When I was a boy, we lived along a sandy hillside field that in odd years held rows of soybeans, and in even years, a crop of corn. There was no real fence between the edges of our yard and the field, but if we'd walk a few feet to the south past our driveway, we'd encounter a rusty old woven wire fence, its locust posts leaning at odd, decrepit angles, like a hag's crooked teeth.

My mom always tossed table scraps and potato peelings near the fence, knowing that when she returned the next day with another bowl of odds and ends, that every crumb would be gone, a possum a bit fatter, a bird or two a bit happier because of it. It was there that we could always look out a window toward the south and east to see a raccoon or a cardinal or a squirrel as they took turns snooping amid the offerings and filling their plates.

I used to walk that fencerow back to the woods

behind our house; I hunted mushrooms along it, took note that it was the poison ivy and the sumacs and the bittersweet that first pulled on fall colors weeks ahead of the oaks and ashes and maples that sat on the other side, but not much in advance of the tulip poplars and sassafras and sycamores. My grandfather often burned the grass and weeds from the fencerows in the spring, but by the time fall rolled around, they'd be fat with saplings and haggard ironweeds and wild roses and the bright yellow flowers of sunchoke. I think he enjoyed watching the fire and smelling the smoke in springtime; he must have liked to stand and lean on a shovel, too.

My friend, Marion Jackson, wrote a piece about such places years ago in "Snowy Egret" magazine. In it, he reminisced about a fencerow from his youth. It was on his southern Indiana "homeplace" and he knew it well. Some 50 years after he played near the spot, he returned there. His brother owned the farm by then, but he had never gotten around to clearing the fencerow, and it made Marion happy.

"I hope he never does [get it cleared]," Jackson wrote. "That old fencerow is one of the few ecological islands surviving in the sea of present-day chemical farming. It is also a reminder of how the rural landscape of southern Indiana once was."

Anyway, I have been taking note of the fencerows near my place lately, all neglected it seems, whether they be mine or those of a neighbor. But while there is always a good view framed by a well-maintained fence, there seems to me a painting created by a fencerow that has been allowed to go back to nature.

As I walked along one night, "picking them up and putting them down," my dad liked to say, I listened to the rattling corn and felt the warm breeze that blew it into a symphony. I noticed that I could look a bit deeper into the woods already, for a good many leaves, dried and dusty from a long, hot summer, have already dropped. A walnut sapling had turned golden, its leaves splotched with rusty holes. Nearby, a patch of blackberry vines held leafy flames of saw-toothed red, all in stark contrast to the bright orange of a stand of scrawny sassafras trees. Amid the whole palette of color sits an even brighter black gum tree, its leaves already piling up at its base.

In the smoky light of dusk, I saw a horde of big, fat dragonflies as they swarmed in perhaps what would be their final dogfight, and even the countless crickets chirping their legs raw in the ditches sounded a bit worn out.

Our summer is about to go away, but those old fencerows will just throw off their summer wear, put on a jacket, and hunker down in anticipation of a north wind. I guess I had better do the same.

———————

The simple beauty of an untended garden
October 17, 2011

I can hear a combine eating its way across a nearby cornfield as I write this on a Saturday evening. It is a sound that signals the end of one season and the beginning of another. The racket of its cutting and shelling isn't as pleasant as those of the soft breezes that catch a wind chime just around the corner from my open window, but it is a necessary noise. Besides, the sound will be a memory in just a few weeks as the fields lose their corn stalk rattles and lay down to sleep for the winter.

I have spent my day outdoors until now. I was up early, my newspaper and coffee consumed in the silence of our kitchen. The quietude soon gave way to the ugly buzz of an old weed trimmer, a saw blade torqued onto its head ready to do battle with fading peonies and scruffy saplings and dried coneflower stalks.

I had told Joanie the night before that I wanted to cut our flower garden to the ground and empty the dregs of the summer planters, their marigolds and petunias now thin and tired and ceding turf to the chrysanthemums. Since I knew the weather was going to be perfect for such chores, I woke earlier than I wanted to, as is a customary irritation with me, with thoughts of rakes and wheelbarrows and pleasant southern winds in my head.

Our flower garden is a dusty little plot of clay that at one time refused to grow much more than a few scruffy thistles and dandelions. The folks who owned our house 30 years ago had the spot fenced off for their horses, that in turn obliged them by trodding the dirt into a bleached and barren wasteland.

Over time, I tore down the old wire fence that kept the horses from peeking into the bedroom windows and pulled its gnawed locust posts for firewood. I planted a grove of red pines that eventually grew to hide and seclude the spot, and I borrowed my folks' tiller and turned a narrow strip of the pasture into powder, slogging behind the moving tines time and time again until I felt I had a perfect garden spot.

At first, I grew vegetables, a little corn and a few tomatoes and a half-dozen rows of green beans. But, despite fertilizing and mulching and weeding and watering, the garden never really produced much, so I eventually worked in a row of Indian corn here and a few pumpkins there and a bed or two of zinnias at each end. Before too long, I had more of a conversation piece than a garden that actually put food on our table.

Over time, the pumpkins and the birdhouse gourds I tried to grow went the way of our vegetables, and I decided we needed a flower garden, instead, that would add color to a relatively colorless lawn, and I went to work again. Using soft sand bricks that Joanie — then pregnant with our daughter — and I culled from an ancient wreck of a farmhouse years ago, I lined a dog's hind leg of a walkway through the garden spot and started dropping seeds both bought and bestowed into the soil. I planted black-eyed

Susans and coneflowers and irises and hollyhocks, and on the shaded end, I dug hole after hole for young hostas I transplanted from the hillsides of my homeplace a few miles away. I planted modest clumps of grasses that today have multiplied themselves times over, and I indiscriminately shoved sedum and mint and butterfly bushes into the mix, too. In time, I had a place filled with pinks and purples and yellows. A spot of lumpy soil that couldn't do much to feed us, and that had no plan to it, was filled with the blooms of summer lilies and the flutter of spicebush and swallowtail butterflies.

It didn't take long for me to realize today that I have neglected my garden this summer. I have mown around it, and walked through it on occasion, pulling a weed here and there, but as the summer and its dryness and its heat wore on, I grew to ignore it. Vines had taken over much of it, and poison ivy had overrun its sunniest corners. I hadn't noticed at all that a pink-berried ground cover had crept up from the woods to infiltrate the place like a silent assassin, and I found mulberries and slippery elms a yardstick tall that had hidden themselves from my pruning shears for months. It was sloppy and weedy, and I was a little ashamed that something that looked good from a distance now seemed so shabby and neglected when seen up close. But I noticed something else, too.

Nearby, a canopy of walnut and cherry trees was dropping a golden shower of leaves, and I often stopped my raking and pulling to just stand and watch it all. I muttered to myself that I was lucky to have such work, for despite my neglect, the garden was filled with color. In its dying, the place had become a collage of deep yellows and ripe reds and rusty browns. The ivy had grown into a variegation of greens and purples, and the grasses, some much taller than I am, had delicate gossamer heads that were tossed in the breeze. The garden was beautiful in a different, simple way.

Today, I acted like that combine down the road, and I mowed my garden down, just as I do each fall. On a day that was as perfect as a day can be — about 80 and breezy and clear — I waded into that patch of earth not expecting to be surprised at all, but I was.

The lizard wore long-johns, and other Halloween tales
October 31, 2011

We stocked our house with a supply of Halloween candy last week; Joanie and I stopped into the new dollar store in town and filled a grocery cart with Butterfingers and Baby Ruths and Three Musketeers bars. Every aromatic bit of it has been calling to me from the orange-and-black baskets we keep on a living room trunk ever since.

As she went for a gallon of milk and a bag of pretzels, she told me to pick out what our visitors might like, and, by coincidence, I figured the little ghouls shared a taste for chocolate and caramel and peanuts with me, and if they don't, I imagine I can find a home for it all. I tossed a bag of Tootsie Pops into the mix, too, quietly hoping that no one but me would like them. As a matter of fact, that bag of goodies hasn't gotten off my desk yet and, unfortunately, it developed a nasty tear that allowed my favorite flavors — cherry and orange — to spill out.

Halloween has become a quieter affair for us over the past few years. My kids aren't kids anymore, at least in a physical sense, so we're no longer loading them into the car and hauling them around in the dark to extort treats from neighbors and friends and family. No Batman capes hanging on the closet door knobs, no Teenage Mutant Turtle masks or face paint to buy anymore, either. We just flip on a porch light and wait for our great nephews and nieces to show up at the door, all still young enough to be holding their parents' hands in silence. I'm sure they'll get the hang of it soon.

I recently read that Americans spend more money celebrating Halloween than any other occasion except Christmas and possibly Super Bowl Sunday. According to a recent Newsweek magazine article, when it is all said and done, we will spend nearly $7 billion in this country on Halloween — more than $2 billion of it on costumes and masks alone. The vast majority of the 1.1 billion tons of pumpkins produced in America is sold for Halloween festivities, and the sales rake in another $150 million.

My brother and sister and I loved Halloween. We come from a long line of strange relatives, and since we were brought up in the tradition of Lon Chaney's "Wolfman" and Boris Karloff's "Frankenstein," we developed a taste for an amalgam of horror and sugar like other all-American kids. My mother, who had an almost zero-tolerance policy toward junk television, inexplicably allowed us to stay up late on weekend nights to watch "Sammy Terry" and his creaking coffin lid on WTTV, Channel 4 out of Bloomington. I suppose it was because the station had a limited budget, but Terry had to make do with a rubber spider, a fog machine, and a pair of black double-knit slacks with a matching turtleneck, along with his purple cape, of course.

I enjoyed the spider, by the way, because my Great-Grandmother Clara used to carry one in her purse, just to entertain us kids. I told you I had a strange family...

Celebrating Halloween in our clan did not require deep pockets. Since we lived too far out of town for any of our school friends to come by our place to trick-or-treat, we usually saw only our cousins come to the door. Their costumes were, most often, the ones that we had worn the year before, or that we would wear the year after, because my grandmother, aunt and mom all got together to mend and patch the outfits from our family pool of hole-filled hats, well-worn masks and seedy sports jackets. Much of it was stored in a musty trunk in my grandpa's garage with my great uncle's World War II bayonet and duffle bag.

Our costumes never really ran to the dark side either — no vampires, no ax-wielding psychopaths. On more than one occasion, I was a lizard ... yes, I did say a lizard. My Grandma Blanche owned an old gargoyle mask, and coordinated with a dyed-green union suit — a tail was sewn to the backside trapdoor — I struck terror into the hearts of neighbors when I leapt through their front doors, a most unimaginative but open brown paper sack in my hands.

My grandmother, who was a deeply spiritual person, still enjoyed Halloween, herself, and saw no devilish connotations to it. She and my mom often donned the rags of hobos, and both wore opaque plastic masks with darkened eyebrows and ruby red lips, their hair tucked under old fedoras. Actually, I found the pair rather creepy.

Our taste for Halloween once led us kids to beg our grandparents into using their coal room — an airless, dank, dungeon of a place in their basement — as a "House of Horrors." Already a grim-looking, Edgar Allan Poe-kind of recess, my sister, Lora, and cousin, Renee, were put in charge of collecting the massive revenue we expected to rake in when the crowds queued in the stairwell to tour it; they never got the memo. "We asked Mom if she would cook spaghetti so we could use it for intestines," my sister recalled, "but she said she needed it for supper."

My sister also reminded me of one of our favorite Halloween haunts: the tiny farm home of the Stahls, who lived up a narrow country lane to our north. They were an old and friendly and wrinkled couple who kept their house somewhere between blast furnace and rocket engine hot, but they actually came across with the goods: chocolate bars and gum, instead of homemade popcorn balls and fruit.

My sister recalled one particular evening when she snagged a Reese's Cup at the Stahls' house. "I couldn't wait to get out of there so I could sink my teeth into that peanut butter and chocolate," she said. "Coming from a poor kid with a bag full of apples, banana moon pies (I still detest those things) and greasy lunch sacks of popcorn, it was a fleeting taste of Heaven."

I think she could be a writer, too...

Obviously, I prefer the Halloweens I had as a kid to the ones I see now. We had to be creative — that happens when you have no money — and there were really no tricks in any of us, regardless of what we were given, even rock candy, which then was sold by the train car load. Sis also remembered a time when we all stood in the rain on one particularly cheap neighbor's doorstep, and only after we were thoroughly soaked were we rewarded with a shiny new dime...

We didn't "corn" cars, never ran toilet paper through our neighbors' trees — even our 10-cent friends — and we never tried to give a local octogenarian a coronary, either. It sounds boring today, I suppose, but despite not having Freddy and Jason, and all of the other mayhem-making creeps to petrify us, we loved it, right down to the rubber spider in Granma Clara's purse.

Now, if you'll excuse me, I have a Tootsie Pop to finish.

In the neighborhood with the 'fantastic' Mr. Fox
November 14, 2011

As we drove home late one night last week, my wife and I, both a bit drowsy and anxious for a warm bed and a long nap, were surprised to see a red fox as it darted across the road. He made his appearance in a flash — just a bit of nose and fur and bushy tail — as he jumped out of a ditch in front of our car and was caught in the glare of our headlights on his way to the relative safety of an apple orchard.

Foxes are not rare in our county at all, but they are rarely seen, so we get a little excited when we spot one. We know that they prowl our place, for we haven't much out here but hills and hollows and trees and spaces that seem to suit them.

Over the years, we have seen foxes that have been killed along our roads, passing them as we've headed into town, only to come back a few hours later to find their tails clipped, the carcasses left for the buzzards. Whoever had stopped to cut the tails gained a talisman of sorts, I suppose, but there was something in their acts that left us cold and more than a bit sorry.

Red foxes (*Vulpes vulpes*) have faced slanderous accusations for years. Regarded in folklore as "sly" and "cunning," as assassins of chickens and turkeys and lambs in real life, and, inexplicably, as manipulative and devilish in the morals of old fables, foxes are actually more adaptive than anything else.

As there are more and more of us humans — a point driven home a few weeks back when it became official that the world's population had turned over 7 billion, give or take a few hundred thousand — there are fewer and fewer of them, although it is known that foxes live both near and in urban areas without causing too much mischief.

There are few reasons for maintaining the fox's bad reputation these days. According to our state's own Department of Natural Resources, it is ground squirrels and mice and song birds that have the most to fear from their red-furred foes. They aren't very large, either; the average adult weighs in at only eight to 14 pounds. Why, we've had heftier housecats than that, although our felines neither work as hard for a meal nor move nearly as quickly.

It is estimated that almost 40 percent of a red fox's diet consists of insects and berries, even leaves. I have no doubt that the fox Joanie and I saw that night was minding his own business. It was less likely that it had been raiding a chicken coop than merely grabbing a rotten apple. Modern husbandry and wire and electric fences and strobe lights have pretty well eliminated the pilfering that foxes became notorious for years ago. They've adapted, and now snoop through dumpsters and compost piles and roadside trash for most of their fast-food fixes.

It was a summer of foxes for me. No less than three times, I drove my truck around a bend in a country road to see one as it slipped into a cornfield or stood motionless watching and sniffing the air before pulling a Houdini and fading into the landscape. In each instance, I considered myself lucky, for I don't see them as often as I do the crows and deer and rabbits that glide over or wander through our property on a daily basis. As with the occasional owl or heron, we feel more privileged by a fox's visit; it's hard to explain, but we do.

There is something mysterious about foxes. According to Martin Wallen, who wrote his book, "Fox," in 2006, all varieties of the animals have worldwide reputations. For instance, it was in Finland that the aurora borealis first became known as "foxfire," for it was believed that a fox running across the sky painted the splendid colors with its tail. In many cultures, the fox was believed to be a shape-shifter, that they most often transformed themselves into conniving women. The Achumawi Indians — who lived primarily in northern California — believed that a silver fox assisted the coyote in "preparing the world for the coming of the first people," ironic since coyotes are most often the prime suspects in fox deaths, that is unless you count those killed by cars.

Of course, we don't appreciate foxes for their exotic history. They are beautiful animals, and their decidedly pedestrian habits make them more at home in open Indiana farm country than just about anywhere else. Despite beliefs to the contrary, foxes are not the den dwellers we suppose them to be. They use dens only when they are rearing youngsters and are mostly solitary creatures, matching up with a mate in the very late fall or early winter. The pair then stays together in a den, and once their pups — usually five or six to a litter and blind for up to two weeks after their births — are weaned (after eight-to-ten weeks), Mom and Dad stick around only long enough to train their clan how to hunt, then pack their bags and go their separate ways.

Even in the coldest of winters, foxes stay out in the open. They often sleep curled into a ball, their fabulous tails wrapped around paws and noses for insulation against the frigid air and snow. They are remarkable athletes, too. According to The Nature Conservancy, foxes can run at speeds up to 30 miles per hour and are capable of leaping 15 feet at a time.

Foxes mostly spend their day trying to stay alive. They are frequently ambushed by larger predators, and, of course, they are hunted and trapped for their coats. In the long run, they may simply lose out to man because of our insistence for taking up their spaces. Foxes may, in fact, need to be sly if they are to survive us.

After our brief encounter along the road, I told my wife that the fox we saw was probably so scared by the experience that he was "still running."

I hope our foxes can run and run for years to come.

———

Persimmons planting a few seeds in our heads for winter

November 28, 2011

Surely, you have heard that we are in for a long, rough winter. The local weather forecasters are saying it; "The Farmer's Almanac" is warning us of it; and now, the persimmons have confirmed it.

It has been said that persimmon seeds have been reasonably accurate winter weather forecasters for years, at least that's what folklorists believe. Just a few weeks back, a local television weatherman showed viewers how to look at a seed to tell whether it will be a mild winter, one known for harsh, bitter, cold, or one best remembered for snowfall. His seeds said snow, and plenty of it.

I stopped in at my mother-in-law's place one day last week. She has three persimmon trees there, old friends who have supplied the fruit that made the pulp that led to a thousand cookies and countless bowls of pudding for our clan over the years. They are non-descript trees, homely in their cragginess, bent like old beggars who live on the northernmost boundary of the lawn, underappreciated and unclimbed now.

By November, when their leaves are just a memory, we see them nearly glow with half dollar-sized fruits. No one picked the persimmons there this year, so when I was finished pulling a small sack's worth in the drizzle and fog that afternoon, I found them smashed into the treads of my boots, as if they were begging to be pulped one way or the other, my size 12s acting as a blender of sorts.

When I was a boy (I know, this sounds like a long, long story), we had a stand of persimmon trees that stood to the south of my Grandpa Roy's garden. We all called the place "The Persimmon Grove," and we played there, for not only those trees grew in the spot, but also a huge oak that held a tree house that my brother, John, and cousin, Roger, had built. It was a special place, not just now as I remember falling out of that tree to end up crying under the glowing lamps of Doc Fell's alcohol-laced examination room in Rosedale, but because my grandfather witched for water there — and found it — and because my grandmother wanted us to grab all the persimmons we could get from it. She was a prodigious canner of almost anything.

Persimmon trees are remarkable things. Most often smallish (two of my mother-in-law's trees stand barely 15 feet or so), they are hardy, can grow in just about any kind of soil (although I think they lean toward sandy dirt), and can produce prodigious amounts of fruit, although they usually wait a year in between big loads. The tree (*Diospyros virginiana*) is dioecious; that is, according to Purdue University, each one produces only either male or female flowers. According to science, trees of both sexes are needed for pollination, and only the female trees bear fruit, but my wife says that the two smaller trees at her old home place have not always been there, and yet the biggest of the trio always yielded persimmons year after year.

Persimmon wood was once highly prized for making the heads of golf clubs, but not these days; metals and resins and plastics have replaced it. I have heard that persimmon was used on occasion for furniture veneers, and I remember an old Rosedale bowl-making friend who used persimmon in some of his work. A friend of another woodworking buddy of mine turns bowls too, and not long ago he told my friend that the roots of persimmon trees are the blackest wood on the continent — "onyx" in fact — and he has turned a beautiful bowl from it.

It is said that splitting a persimmon seed to peek inside is a surefire winter weather indicator. A spoon-shaped pattern in the meat of the seed means snow; a fork means a mild winter; a knife suggests a season of bitter winds and moody cold. The last time I had seen the annual seed-splitting ritual was in my persimmon grove days, my grandfather slicing through the slimy black-grey seed with his pocketknife. Partially out of curiosity, partly out of homage to old times, I decided to do the same thing in my kitchen.

The persimmons I yanked had seen their better days; a few frosts had reduced them to shriveled orange versions of Moms Mabley (old Ed Sullivan Show reruns will help with that analogy), much of their pucker power already shivered out of them. They were soft with thickish hides, and more than a few literally held their pulp like eggs hold yolks.

Our persimmons were not short on seeds either. Each small globe of fruit held at least five or six. The trees themselves can be grown from grafted roots, but nature prefers to do it the old-fashioned way. One tree produces so many seeds, you'd think persimmons would be everywhere, yet they aren't that commonly found.

For my experiment, I took out my wife's cutting board, gave a selected seed a good washing, then held the thing between the jaws of a pair of good pliers. I remember watching my television friend do his slicing, and I felt a bit uneasy when I considered what his knife would do to his fingers as he held the slippery target.

I used my dad's "Buck Henry," the sharpest knife I own, and I slowly sawed into the seed as if I were opening an oyster. What I found amazed me; the very first seed held a spoon-shaped outline, nearly as big as the seed's core, and it stared at me from the kitchen counter, its proportion suggesting I'll need a snow plow this winter rather than a snow shovel.

A few days after I split the seed, a little like Fermi split the atom, I found myself rummaging through my clothes closet. It has been a windy fall, so blustery in fact that I had a feeling that even had the persimmons disagreed, winter might show up a little earlier than in most years. So, I decided that it was probably wise to take stock of my long underwear and boot socks and scarves.

According to the experts — persimmons included

— it might not be a bad idea to have my insulated boots and that snow shovel ready too.

Violets in October, a pleasant surprise
October 15, 2012

I guess I don't pay much attention to the weather forecasts these days because it surprised me a bit when our furnace kicked on a few nights ago. I am by nature a cheap man, which explains why I dial our thermostat back far enough that only Iditarod-worthy temperatures finally get our registers to crackle and the warmth of gas flames to flicker in our house.

This fall seems to be in a bit of a hurry. Just a few days ago, I still sported both tanned arms and open windows, yet, just yesterday, I had to move a half-a-dozen long-sleeved shirts into my bedroom closet from the one where we keep our out-of-season clothes. I have been rummaging around for boot socks and sweatshirts and flannel "leisure wear," too, and the space heater in my bathroom has sure felt good lately.

Autumn brings out the writer in me, it seems. There is something about crisp blue skies and brisk north winds that inspire me to put words on paper, mostly, I suppose, because I am always surprised at how quickly, and how beautifully, the world can change. One minute, I am sweating away at trimming shrubs and grabbing crabgrass by the handfuls; then, virtually overnight, I am sticking chrysanthemums in the ground and blowing yellow maple leaves off my deck, and moving potted plants under the barn's eaves to keep them from the mean fingers of frost. I shouldn't still be surprised by those things at my age, but I am.

I guess the first day I knew that autumn was seriously considering residency came a few weeks ago. I was driving home from work, a bit lost in my own thoughts.

The windows were down on my truck, and I was enjoying the sun on my arms, and I was thinking about what I wanted to do when I got home, that is after I had a bite to eat and a glance at the junk we still call mail. Just before I came into the little burg just north of my house, I looked to the east and saw the sun playing tag with a field that has in the past few years become overgrown with a healthy crop of goldenrod and cottonwood saplings. Those few acres literally danced with every shade of yellow and gold imaginable, and I felt better about my day then and there.

A good friend, who often writes to me, said one day last week that she was surprised to have discovered violets in her yard. "Imagine that," she wrote, "violets in October." But I didn't have to imagine it; as I pushed a mower along a hillside near my flower garden the very evening I got her note, I saw perfectly purple little violets growing there, too.

The soybeans in the field across from us are soon to be cut, as are the fields of bedraggled corn along the roads we walk nearly year-round; I saw the dust of the combines this evening. The yields aren't supposed to be very good this year, but they might surprise us. Joanie and I have gotten into the habit of wandering off our roadside walks into the corn, just to check an occasional ear. Some have surprised us with their uniformity and size. The stalks may look terrible — thin, emaciated things that are already leaning in the breeze — but I am amazed at how that corn and those beans could go so long without even a sip of water and still have anything to show for it.

It may be the cooler nights, but our geraniums seem to be going out in a blaze of glory, too. I don't think the blooms in the stone flowerbeds near our barn and in the brown clay pots just below my cabin have looked as good all summer as they do right now. I see them framed through my cabin window, and I think of an Andrew Wyeth painting that I am a little too lazy to search for in one of my art books. I know I have that picture, but Wyeth's palette has nothing on the real thing.

I have been surprised that our dry, dry summer hasn't cut into our walnut and hedge apple harvest, too, but we still seem to have them both by the bushel. I have thought the trees would have conserved themselves by producing only what is necessary, but such was not the case. The grass in my yard has come back from the dead, too, resurrected by the fall rains like Lazarus. Now, it seems to be saying to me, "You've saved your labor and gasoline and time long enough, so I'll make you mow until dark, even well into November, if need be."

We are beginning to see full fall color in our trees, and that, too, is unexpected. Most people I know who care about such things believed that our drought would lead to fast-falling piles of brown, trashy leaves, but our sassafras trees have been lit up as if covered with orange and red Christmas tree lights. Just a few days ago, my wife and I were hiking back to the house, and we saw a bright orange maple poking a glowing head up above our tree line. I can't say I have ever noticed that tree looking so gaudy.

We've had other surprises: rogue cantaloupes that grew beneath the ornamental grass near my cabin, their starter seeds undoubtedly planted there by some careless bird; pine needles falling by the wheelbarrow load from a white pine that looked a little peaked and tired all summer; and, just this past weekend, a handful of warm, wet days that blew in from the south.

But perhaps the most pleasant surprise I have had thus far this fall came as I worked in the back yard a week ago. I was raking a windy day's worth of walnut hulls and twigs off our back hill, and the breeze sprinkled me with a wonderful shower of gold and red wild cherry leaves. Perhaps I need a hobby, maybe I'm easily entertained, but things like that seem to make me smile before they take up residence in my head for a while.

On a recent night, I sat in my family room recliner, a baseball game playing on the television as I graded a few tests with waning enthusiasm. The game didn't involve my beloved Red Sox; they didn't make the playoffs this fall. In fact, they finished dead last in their division. Now that I think of it, that's no surprise at all...

Growing up and old with so many to feed
October 29, 2012

At our family reunion last summer, I asked my brother if I could borrow a pair of photo albums he had put together. Over the past couple of years, I have committed quite a few of our family's old yellowing snapshots to newly cropped and digitalized lives, and I wanted to do the same with some of the pictures John has collected for himself.

As I thumbed through the albums just a few days later, I caught myself stopping at times to remember the voices and the laughter of my parents and grandparents, my aunts and uncles, and even a cousin or two who have left us over the years. We miss them, and so, besides our memories, those photos are nearly all we have left to connect with our pasts.

Near the back of one of the collections was a picture of my big brother and me; he is holding a little dog on his lap, and all three of us are looking straight into a camera that was undoubtedly held by my mom. We are shirtless and sitting on our back step; the picture had to have been taken nearly 50 summers ago.

That photo reminded me of something my cousin, Renee, told me at that same reunion. She and her brothers,

Rick and Roger, grew up in a house just across the County Line Road from us, and because my grandparents lived a few hundred yards up a shared driveway to the west, our family never really stayed in just one house, but rather shared three. She told me that in virtually every childhood picture she had ever seen of my brother and sister, Lora, and me, there was always a dog or a cat in our arms or at our feet. "You always had something to feed," she said with a smile.

I suppose that's true. My mom was not one to turn away an empty stomach from the door, whether it be human or feline or canine. So, as we grew up, then moved on to houses of our own to make livings and raise families, we took that love of the furred and fanged and pawed with us. My brother and sister and I are all still feeding something, and so are my two kids.

In the young years we spent on that sandy, hilly bit of earth, my family fed quite a menagerie of animals. We had a stocky Welsh pony named Dusty and a dusty old mule name Rosie, and we often kept a few cattle (one named T-Bone that I still don't like to speak about) and sheep to graze the two or three fenced acres we had just behind the house. We, of course, always had dogs, and although the name of the pup in that old photo with John has long escaped the two of us, I can't help but remember our collie. She was a stray who came to stay, and in a moment of no apparent imagination, we named her Lassie, of course. Lassie was a fidgety neurotic that hated storms.

In fact, she'd claw the back door off the house at the first rumble of thunder, and since my mom was no fan of wind and lightning herself, I remember a number of nights when we coaxed the dog down our steep basement steps so she could join us until a tempest had blown through.

Not long after Lassie came to us, I had the misfortune of finding out just how hungry she always was, even after enjoying a few months at our table with a steady diet of table scraps and dog food. I remember walking out of the back door of our house — it was my birthday — and in short pants and untucked shirt, I carefully balanced a fat piece of cake on a plate and held a slopping cup of milk. I was headed across the driveway to our swing set, but Lassie wanted the cake too, and as she jumped up to take a look, I jerked away from her, but not before she got ahold of a bit of the rather chubby stomach that I had failed to tuck in. I forgave her, despite the fact that, after a dramatic trip into Rosedale with Dad, Doc Fell liberally employed the use of Methiolate, and his hypodermic needle, which seemed as fat as a pencil.

Over the years, I became buddies with two old tomcats named Smokey Joe and Kitty Tom, another mutt named Cina, a crow, two skunks and literally hundreds of fish (including a piranha) and birds (parakeets and parrots and even a cockatiel) that John managed to keep in cages, tanks and roosts on our back porch, and, much to my mom's dismay, in our utility room.

We had a pet raccoon, too. His name was Sammy

(named, for some reason, after Sammy Terry, the late-night TV ghoul), and we raised him on a bottle. My grandfather, a well-known raccoon killer, had dispatched Sammy's mother on one of his forays into the woods behind us, but unable to leave a baby — no heavier than a spoon — behind, he brought him to my mom, who soon had him riding her dust mop and eating breakfast at a cat dish in the kitchen. Sammy eventually insisted on living outdoors. I still remember how bitterly Mom cried when he died on the busy road in front our house, undoubtedly returning home from a feast on the fat, brown crawdads that lived on the other side.

My Grandfather Roy always had hunting dogs, and one in particular, named Matt (yes, as in "Gunsmoke's" he-man marshal), became his favorite. I spent a lot of time riding in my grandpa's truck, Matt in the middle of us, very much looking like a homely old man with a dirty face. In the meantime, my cousins had Flip, a three-legged dog, reduced to a tripodal life by a run-in with a woven-wire fence. He came over to our house every day, carefully looking both ways before he headed across the road.

This night, a warm breeze is blowing in my open window, although it is probably going to be one of the last times I can say that for a while. I have been thumbing through those photo albums again, for I promised weeks ago that I'd give them back to my brother the next time I saw him. But I have mostly been thinking about the countless cats and pooches that we have fed over the years, found homes for over the years, kept and loved over the years.

Sure, they've all been "something to feed," but we know, they were more than that. I'm glad we took pictures.

Reflections on a bit of red glass and our daily thanksgivings
November 12, 2012

I sat in the half-light of my old desk lamp a few nights ago, a chilly wind blowing in from the northwest that made me appreciative of my cotton sweater and purring heater. I had come to my cabin for a little quiet, not really much of a departure from the usual state of our house, for our kids are grown and gone, and my wife and I live in a comfortable and mutually imposed peacefulness that is rarely broken by sounds we don't invite inside.

I just wanted to sit amidst my books and papers and accumulated odds and ends to think and listen to nothing in particular, and that I accomplished. It was after only a few minutes of solitude that I spied a bit of red glass sitting on a window ledge that runs from west to east alongside my desk. With it resides an arrowhead and a chunk of fossilized wood that I found in childhood adventures so long ago that even the memories of them have been worn smooth by time.

There's a ceramic jar, decorated with green dragonflies, on the ledge too. In it are a hodgepodge of pens and pencils, a few of which I never use, but since they look nice in their repose in the jar, I've decided to just leave them where they are.

The talisman in question is polished and nearly oval, and it's as colorful as the handmade glass cardinal I keep perched on the ledge too. It's as if it has spent time in a rock tumbler, turned over and over until there's no hint of a sharp edge. It holds only recent memories, for it was given to me by Carmen Palma, a proper little lady with whom we attend church. Calling it a "Thankful Stone," Carmen passed a small wicker basket of the glass baubles from pew to pew a few years back, telling those of us at that Sunday morning devotion to pick one of the color and size we wanted. She told us that we should put the "stone" somewhere close at hand so that when we see it we'll be reminded to be thankful, to be grateful for what and who we have in our lives. I did so, and more than a few times I have looked at that little piece of glass catching the sunlight, and I've remembered Carmen's words, for like most of us, I'm not as appreciative as I should be.

My wife took a red stone too. She placed it on the oak ledge that runs under our kitchen greenhouse window, and she has told me that on occasion, as she washed a pot or pan at the sink, or sliced a bowl of apples or onions, that she noticed the glass sparkling in the sun, and she's tried to think of something or someone for which she was grateful, a tough chore if you knew just how tired she often is, and how late she works at that spot.

I know that this story comes to you a week or so

before Thanksgiving, but I couldn't help but spread Carmen's message today, not because I heed it daily myself, but because I so often forget to, grumbling and mumbling about what I don't own, or where I can't go, or what I can't do. I have had a week filled with such frumpiness, prompted, I suppose, by long hours at work and endless chores, a congested head, and cool, cloudy November days that have draped themselves over me like a wet wool blanket.

Taking stock, I have to admit that I have very little to complain about. My family is healthy and happy, and nary a sibling nor offspring, nor even distant cousin, as far as I know, has to give a second thought about being warm or well fed or unemployed. I have a job, my bills are paid, and I know that I'm loved, despite the way I act at times. I know too, that even though there is always a chance of big winds blowing or high water rising or deep snow falling here in this weatherman's headache we call the Midwest, that I am much better off than so many of those who live along the East Coast, the victims of not one monster storm, but two that have compounded their miseries.

It was quite a leap to make as I rolled the glass over in my palm to that of another story I heard years ago. I have never hiked the sharp, craggy valleys of the Scottish Highlands, except when I've read Robert Louis Stevenson or listened to my brother, who visited there once, but I have heard that there is a stone — a much larger and more authentic one than the one that sits on my window sill —

at an intersection of two roads along the western shore of Loch Lomond. It was placed there by the soldiers who built it in 1753.

Although the original marker fell into ruin, a replacement has always been in place. Greeting the weary and travel-worn, although more of a tourist attraction now that people motor past on their way to other places, the stone's inscription reads simply: "Rest and Be Thankful."

I need to be better at remembering to be thankful, even in the simplest of times: when I am listening to a Copland symphony; when I smell the scent of fallen leaves; when I feel content as I sit with a book and watch the snow fall into my woods; when I am at work; when I hear my son or daughter walk through our back door. Thankful when I think of all who've served this country in the military; for the memories of my parents; for the first time I hear frogs calling from the pond over our back hill ...

On Thanksgiving Day, I hope I take the time to remember these things, and when the day has passed, I'll still have that red stone on my window ledge as a reminder to me the rest of the year.

A library, even a little one, is a good thing
October 1, 2012

I grew up with libraries, and I can't imagine there ever being a time when I won't want to wander one exploring it like some bookworm-Balboa, finding an author or title that I never really knew existed before. Creating those "Eureka" moments seems to be a dying interest now that so many of us download and digest books electronically without ever really considering that there just might be some hidden gem we'd have liked even more had we simply stumbled upon it on a shelf by accident. I think those moments of discovery are not unlike kicking up lost treasure a mile from where X marks the spot.

My wife feels the same way, and because we live near a little town, and in the end of a very rural county that has no public library within a decent drive, we already knew we wanted the children who are growing up around us to have access to books, as we so fortunately did when we were young.

We reasoned that the local elementary school library is always closed for the summer, its chairs stacked on their backs like dead crickets, its books gathering dust. So, last week, with the help of a few friends — one in particular — we planted a little library in the sandy soil of Rosedale proper, near the Dollar General Store. We hope it's used year-round, though, for it'll never really be closed.

Joanie and I first learned about the "Little Free Library" movement early last spring by watching television. The whole story reminds me of what Groucho Marx once said of TV: "I find television very educating. Every time somebody turns on the set, I go into the other room and read a book."

But in this case, we both stayed in the room and watched, and what we saw inspired us to try to get others to read books.

Anyway, just before Groucho broke into my thoughts, I was about to say that we knew, even as the news segment that we watched that night was still running, we wanted to make a nice rustic box, set it on a sturdy post in a place where kids would see it, fill it with books, then hope that the words and pictures inside magically disappeared, only to reappear a few days later. It will make us very happy if things go as planned.

As I often do with projects that involve saws and angles and wood, I turned to my friend, Joe Huxford, carpenter, digger of post holes, and all-around good egg. When I told Joe what we wanted to do, he said he'd love to collaborate — he often works on my kooky ideas for no more than a trip to a decent restaurant — and almost immediately we were sending drawings and photos and building material ideas back and forth like a couple of eager kids trading baseball cards. I think I even passed along a few scribbled notions to him on the back of an envelope.

Before Joe could really start construction, however, his youngest son, Jeff, was seriously injured in an automobile accident. Knowing that a woodworking project undertaken on my own would end up better used as fireplace kindling come December, and that Joe's cluttered workshop was to be closed and quiet for a while, I decided to wait. After a long, hot summer, Jeff recovered, and Joe resumed construction in August, quickly and efficiently and creatively completing the library well under budget. That is, since he used scraps of cedar and siding from his shop and my barn loft, the most expensive thing Joe invested in was a pair of bargain-table door hinges.

Oh, he tried to spend some money, but a few good people, who, once they heard what we were doing, decided to chip in too. First, the nice folks at Professional Glass in Clinton — who have expertly framed more than a few things for my walls — gave Joe the library's front door glass. Later, Pastore Brothers Lumber, a rock's throw down Ninth Street from PG, took the grand sum of a dollar for an aluminum starter strip that was needed for the library's roof. Of course, the good people at the Dollar General were involved too; it took only two calls to their corporate office to get the permission we needed. Shannon and Denise and Kris, who pretty well run the place in town, all thought the library to be a grand idea too. "Our kids need to be reading books," Denise told me as she rang up a customer the night we installed the library.

Repeated sprayings of whatever weather sealants Joe had left on his shelves, a bag of concrete and a heavy six-inch-by-six-inch treated post that used to support my mom's birdfeeder later, and our library was up and running in just a few hours. Joanie proudly polished the glass, then unloaded books just as the sun was setting. After all, she's the librarian in the family.

While we were working that night, me arranging a few stones around the library's base, Joanie working at the wiping and cleaning that leftover wood glue and sawdust require, two young boys on bicycles happened by the library. "What's that?" one asked her. "It's a library," she said as he mumbled the words on the sign we had placed below the door. "Take a book; leave a book," he read.

"Couldn't somebody just steal the books," he asked my wife.

"They could," she told him, "But we hope they do the right thing and leave them for somebody who wants to read them." She added, "Most often, I think people do the right thing."

I agree with her about that, and I wholeheartedly believe one other line that we placed on our library's sign too. It reads: "A book is a gift you can open up again and again."

The little man who came to dinner
November 26, 2012

My seven-year-old nephew, Carson, came to visit us last week. That in itself isn't earth-shattering news, for he often drops by with one of his parents or the other, the last time dressed as a ghoul for Halloween. But for a couple like Joanie and me, whose youngest child is now nearly two decades past Carson's age, having a little guy like him in the house, even for a few hours, takes a bit of adjusting.

My wife and I are "empty-nesters" in only the technical sense of the phrase. We loved having our kids at home with us, even encouraged them to stay an extra year or two on our dole while they finished up college. But, for most part, we're too busy, and too happy, I think, to still be pining about the good old days when we were wiping jelly-smeared faces, tying shoestrings, and telling our kids to blow harder. There's little doubt that we'd love to do that all over again if we could, but Carson also reminded us that night that it takes a lot of energy and a lot of effort to raise an active little guy like he is.

He may very well be our "grandparent-in-waiting training," so perhaps we had better have him over again soon.

My sister-in-law and Carson had to shout to get my attention as they caught me blasting leaves over my back hillside with a noisy power blower near dark that evening. I remembered that Joanie had told me that he was going to be with us a couple of hours, but only when I saw him with a box of plastic soldiers in his hands did I realize that it was the appointed day and time. Joanie wasn't home from work yet, and since the sun was already giving up the ghost for the day, I told his mom to have him go on in the house while I cleaned up my tools and knocked the mud off my boots.

It was just a minute or two later, as I washed my dirty hands at our hydrant, that I realized that we no longer had child-safety locks on our cabinets, that my prescription medicine was on the kitchen counter, and that we had several bottles of drain cleaners and other nasty toxins on the shelves under our kitchen sink. I couldn't remember at what time we no longer had to worry about our kids getting into such hazards, so I wiped my wet paws on my jeans, threw my leaf blower in the barn, and headed inside, certain that Carson was already sticking fork tines into electrical outlets, or fiddling with the switch box, or guzzling furniture polish.

I found him, sitting in a chair, petting our cat, Edgar (Carson refers to him as "Egger"), the television blank, the house slightly dark and a bit cold, since I'd not bothered to turn on lights and adjust the thermostat when I came home. No blaring cartoons, no toxic cocktails, no matches, no tipping over the aquarium; Carson was just sitting in the chair, wiggling his feet and very much minding his own business.

Because I was nearly out of gasoline for my mowers, I told him that we could climb into the truck and head to town for refills. Surely, riding in my pickup, operating the gas pump, and watching men spit at the local station would be a hoot for a first grader. Backing out of the drive and heading south toward town reminded me so much of doing the same thing a thousand times with my son or daughter in the seat next to me. We chatted about this and that, Carson responding to my questions with shrugs and rolled eyes and "I don't knows." Twenty bucks worth of unleaded and two spittle-laced howdys from those going in and coming out the station door later, and Carson and I were pulling into the drive to see that Joanie had the house lit and warming.

Joanie kept Carson company for a while because I had a shower to take and two piles of school papers to tackle, but once those chores were dispensed of, we all sat around the supper table together, said our prayer, and filled our plates. Carson was not a big fan of the turkey and gravy and mashed potatoes that Joanie had prepared for us, but he gave two thumbs up to a microwaved hot dog left over from my last dalliance with our gas grill. He wasn't enamored with our corn and green beans either, but he did eventually want the potatoes, that is as long as he could use our pepper grinder to spice things up. Carson is a big fan of pepper. In fact, I began to wonder if there were potatoes under his pepper.

When Joanie asked him what he had his eye on for Christmas, Carson surprised us by saying he wanted, "Dominoes, Dominoes, and more Dominoes!" He didn't know that Dominoes constituted an actual game; he wants to set them, on end, one after another, then tip them over "like the guy on 'America's Got Talent.'" I had to admit, that does sound fun.

I don't know if it was that question, or if he was high on pepper, or the fact that Carson's energy level picked up at about the same time mine was drooping, but from that point on, we got along famously. It had been years since I had a 7-year-old boy to pal around with — the last time I was with my son we both used chainsaws. But I keep a lot of things in my house that are of a natural interest to little guys: ball gloves and books and rocks and pictures and pocket knives, and Carson managed to ask me a question about almost every one of them. In particular, he liked a piece of purple quartz that I keep on my desk with other odds and ends. He likes the fossils and arrowheads and bits of driftwood and feathers I leave around my place, but that quartz, and then a tall jar of white, milky pieces, really caught his eye. I told him that he could have a piece of the quartz, and after fingering through no less than 50 specimens, he selected one for himself.

"I want to go out and see your cabin," Carson told me, the quartz in hand (his mom told me he slept with it a few nights), so since Joanie was still nearly knee-deep in dishes, and we've never used television as a baby sitter, we headed out the back door.

Carson is an interesting, and interested little dude. He wanted to see copies of the books I'd written, wanted to know who the people who stared back at him through picture frames and from beneath the glass on my writing table were. He thought the warm air from my heater "felt good" on his hands, and he asked questions, a lot of questions: "Where'd you get that fish? Does that old radio work? What is your favorite book? "Do you ever sleep out here?" In all, we stayed well over an hour, Carson telling me that of all the books I had on my shelves he wanted to have one in particular, an old Alistair MacLean thriller, which I'll give to him when he's old enough to read it.

When we got back to the house, I thought I could convince Carson to play some kind of game that required us to sit in a recliner and shut our eyes. Instead, he headed to the quartz jar and told me, "I think I like another piece in there better." I told him he should just flip a coin to make the decision as to which piece he liked best. After one flip of the dime (he found me to be an expert flipper, so I was involved), he thought three tosses would be better, then five, then seven. ... Sixty-four flips later, he chose the piece he took out of the jar the first time.

By the time Carson left a little later, still energetic, still full of questions, I was ready for a good book and a warm bed. I waved goodbye as he headed out the door to the car, and I told him to come back anytime.

I think I need to double up on my vitamins first, though.

Also by
MIKE LUNSFORD

The Off Season:
The Newspaper Stories of Mike Lunsford
ISBN 978-0-615-23811-1
Read 51 of the author's earliest stories from his award-winning front page newspaper column. Emmy winner and author Phil Gulley said: "If we could distill, bottle, and distribute Mike Lunsford's good sense, our world would be better for it."

Sidelines:
The Best of the Basketball Stories
ISBN 978-0-615-30731-2
This collection holds over 60 stories about the people, places, and things that make Indiana a basketball heaven. Nationally-known author Randy Roberts says, "Lunsford reminds me of why I love Indiana."

A Place Near Home:
More Stories From The Off Season
ISBN 978-0-615-49749-5
A collection of 59 more stories that prompted columnist Kevin Cullen to say, "Mike's essays are love letters, hymns to family, friends, quiet walks, and all that is good, true, and permanent."